Elias John Wilkinson Gibb

The Story of Jewad

A Romance

Elias John Wilkinson Gibb

The Story of Jewad
A Romance

ISBN/EAN: 9783744693431

Printed in Europe, USA, Canada, Australia, Japan

Cover: Foto ©Thomas Meinert / pixelio.de

More available books at **www.hansebooks.com**

THE STORY OF JEWĀD

THE

STORY OF JEWĀD

A ROMANCE

BY

'Alī 'Azīz Efendi
the Cretan

TRANSLATED FROM THE TURKISH

BY

E. J. W. GIBB, M.R.A.S.

MEMBRE DE LA SOCIÉTÉ ASIATIQUE DE PARIS; AUTHOR OF
Ottoman Poems, ETC.

GLASGOW
WILSON & McCORMICK, SAINT VINCENT STREET
1884

CONTENTS.

PREFACE.

PREFIXED to the little volume from which
the following tale has been extracted, is a
short notice to the effect that on the back of
the manuscript from which the book was
printed, were a few lines stating that 'Alī
'Azīz Efendi of Crete completed his *Mukhayyalat-i Ledun-i Ilahi* in the year of the
Hijra 1211 (A.D. 1796-7), that he died two
years later in 1213 (1798-9), while on a
diplomatic mission in Prussia, that he was
eminent in mysticism, philosophy, and all
the sciences, that he compiled several treatises
on these, containing likewise the convincing
solutions he afforded to the difficult questions
propounded by European savants ; but that
his heirs, ignorant of the value of his writings,
destroyed all save a few which fell into the
hands of certain of his friends who could

appreciate their worth, and who in conse-
quence gave them to the world.

The volume entitled *Mukhayyalat-i Ledun-i
Ilahi*, a name which may be rendered by
'Phantasms from the Divine Presence,' consists of three distinct stories, each styled a
Mukhayyal or 'Phantasm.' All three have
several secondary tales, as is the case in so
many Eastern works of fiction. The first
Mukhayyal consists for the most part of a
series of incidents taken from various romances in The Thousand and One Nights, and
woven together into a connected whole.
There is little alteration in the tales as here
presented, save in the proper names. The
second and longest *Mukhayyal* is the story
of Jewād. The third, a very good story,
contains the wonderful adventures of an
Egyptian prince called Nājī-bi-'llāh and his
son Dil-i Agāh.

The collection seems to have been made
with the view of exalting the Occult Sciences
as practised by the Dervishes. In the first
tale Prince Asīl, by virtue of a talisman, be-

comes King of the Jinn; in the second, the youthful Jewād, a professed magician, is shown forth as the possessor of every virtue; and in the third, a learned and pious Sheykh causes Prince Dil-i Agāh, while in a trance of brief duration, to experience all the vicissitudes of fortune, and to come through a number of marvellous adventures which appear to last over a long period.

I have chosen for translation the Story of Jewād, not only because it is in itself the most interesting of the three, but because it shows the most clearly in what light the Occult Sciences and their practitioners used to be regarded in Turkey. It further contains more details concerning magic ceremonies and Oriental spiritualism than either of the others. An additional interest is imparted to the tale by the fact that at least a portion of it, that describing the hero's doings in Constantinople, gives (the magic apart) a good idea of a section of life in the Ottoman capital about the close of last century. The *naïveté* with which Jewād, who,

b

as already said, is a model of all the virtues, directs his friend Ibrāhīm Chelebi to out-bribe the other competitors for the Collector-ship of Aleppo, bears striking witness to the state of official corruption by which the Empire was undermined before the days of the modern reforms.

Seeing that the first *Mukhayyal* is made up of adaptations from The Thousand and One Nights, it is not improbable that the plots of the several stories of the second and third may in like manner be borrowed from some other Arabic or Persian collection. However, those here presented will, I think, in any case be new to most readers, as they are to myself. The only incidents I recollect having met with elsewhere are the dream of Ferah-Nāz, and the voyage of Qara Khān. Of these, the first is practically identical with the Lady Dunyā's dream in The Thousand and One Nights story of Tāju-'l-Mulūk, while the second bears some resemblance to the opening part of the adventures of the Third Qalender.

In the translation (which I have made as literal as possible) I have adopted, in part, at least, a rather antiquated style as being more suited to represent that of the original ; for although the work was written so late as the end of last century it was too early to come under the influence of the great and striking change which has for some years been revolutionising the whole spirit and form of Ottoman literature.* Taking for models the writers of France, as their pre-decessors took those of Persia, the Turkish authors of to-day have elaborated a style utterly unlike anything to be found in the older literature, which had remained com-paratively little altered from the fourteenth century till the time of the great literary re-former, Shināsī Efendi, who died in 1871. This new style, which is much truer and simpler than the ornate and frequently far-

---

* In accordance with the system adopted in my *Ottoman Poems*, all the phrases which in the original occur in Arabic are printed in italics in the translation.

fetched and obscure bombast which passed
for fine writing in the olden time, seems to be
altogether better suited to the Ottoman genius;
at least if we may judge from the remark-
able group of brilliant writers who have
arisen in Turkey since its introduction. Of
these it will be sufficient to mention Munīf
Pasha, the statesman and scholar ; Ekrem
Bey, the poet and Professor of Literature at
the Civil College ; 'Abdu-'l-Haqq Hāmid
Bey, the dramatist; and finally, Kemāl Bey,
who is acknowledged, by general consent, to
be the greatest author of modern Turkey.

It may perhaps be as well to state that the
following words, which in the translation
appear in conjunction with proper names,
are not in themselves names, but titles :—
Shah, Khan, Khoja, Chelebi, Monla, Agha,
Efendi, Khānim, Chawush, Baba, Sheykh,
Emīr. Of these, Shah and Khan are royal
styles (the one Persian, the other Tartar,)
and mean 'King'; Khānim is 'Lady'; Baba,
'Father,' is given to dervishes.

THE STORY OF JEWĀD.

*In the Name of God, the Merciful, the
Compassionate.*

THERE was in Athens, the city of the sages,
a prosperous merchant, Lebīb by name, who,
in the port of the trade of fortune, was en-
nobled with wealth and possessions and
enriched with all manner of worldly goods.
But by reason of his having no son to
succeed him, he was exceeding sad and
mournful; and as the years of his life had
reached seventy, he had at length cut the
thread of hope of the possibility of offspring,
and unloosed the cord of disappointment
and despondency. One day a resplendent
person came forth from among the travellers,
and, after the salutation, seated himself
beside Lebīb. After he had gone through

the ceremony of asking how he fared, the
stranger, having watched for a fitting time,
opened the mouth of wisdom, and thus
began to speak :—" My master, is your
honoured name Lebīb, and was your father's
name 'Adnān, and your mother's Libāba,
and is your wife's Zāhida, and was her
father's Nu'mān, and her mother's Nā'ila ? "
Lebīb was amazed at his question, and said,
" Whence have you known it ? " The
stranger replied : " My master, I, your servant, am Ebū-'Alī Sīnā, and of the learned
sages and renowned philosophers. As to
visit this City of Wisdom is incumbent upon
the endeavours of sages, for the end to
observe the rule of the ancients I have been
for some days a sojourner in your city. Our
wont is abstinence and celibacy ; but when
viewing the splendours of the city, a thought
such as this filled my mind : we can
leave no trace on earth ; would that, being
wedded, we might at least have sons and
grandsons, that the remembrance of us might
remain for a little time in this world of

decay. Saying to myself, 'Had I been wedded, should I have had children?' I sought in the almanack the decrees of my ruling star. I found that I should have had no offspring, but that a boy, Jewād* by name, will be born to you, and that he will be my spiritual son—one learned in the stars and their ascensions ; and my heart was comforted." Then he drew forth from his breast a box and took thereout two pills, and said : " Husband and wife, do ye each eat a pill ; and, *if it please God (exalted be He !)*, when your son has reached his fourteenth year, I pray you send him for his education to me, your loyal friend, at Antioch." Then he arose and departed.

Lebīb marvelled exceedingly at this great good news, and was glad. Straightway he hastened to his home and did according as the sage had commanded ; and when the full time was come, he was rejoiced by the birth of the promised boy, and they called

* Jewād means " Beneficent " ; it is not an uncommon name in Turkey.

his name Jewād, even as the sage had
bidden.

When he had passed through childhood
and attained the age of youth, the noble
Jewād, having heard the story, formed a love
for Ebū-'Alī from what they said. So, un-
dazzled by the vain material wealth of his
parents, he bade farewell to his father and
his mother, and, receiving their blessing, set
out with their permission for his master's
land.   In a short time he was rejoiced by
meeting with Ebū-'Alī.   All his time was
given to the acquisition of science, and Ebū-
'Alī instructed him in various kinds of knowledge ; and, by lavishing on him every care
and attention, he made Jewād so wise a
master and so wondrous a philosopher, that
the saying " An able disciple becomes more
a master than the master" beamed forth
from his brow.

As the talent of Jewād was manifest to
his master, one day, when by reason of the
violence of the rain they had forborne to go
to the college of instruction, and, nothing

being to do in the house, were sitting alone, engaged in pleasant converse, there came a knocking at the door. Ebū-'Alī said to Jewād, " Go, see who knocks at the door." So Jewād went and opened the door, but seeing no one, turned in again, when, lo! what he sees is no longer the house of Ebū-'Alī, but a kingly palace. " *Glory to God !* " he cried, "what has befallen me?" And while he yet stood bewildered in the middle of the court, some forty or fifty slave-girls, beautiful and lovely, covered with gold and all manner of magnificent raiments and ornaments and decorations, descended the steps, and taking Jewād under the armpits,* and saying, " Welcome, and fair welcome, my master," they seated him in a lofty pavilion in an upper storey of the palace. They brought him coffee and tobacco in begemmed cup and pipe ; and when he had finished, two of the slave-girls, taking him as before, conducted him to a delightful and splendid

---

* Such was the manner in which persons of rank used to be ceremoniously conducted.

dressing-room. They stript him of the sage's clothes that were on his shoulders and girded him with gold - embroidered towels, and placed him in a bath, which, when he entered, he saw to be a beautiful bath, the dome whereof was as the vault of heaven, and the windows as the flashing stars. Lovely slave-girls, formed as it were of camphor or crystal, girt with simple towels, reverently and respectfully performed for him the bath-attendants' service. Poor Jewād was bewildered, for never in all his life had he seen or heard of such a bath or such fair frames, inciting the passions ; but he let not the rein of continence and virtue slip from his hand, nor cast a look of desire. So when they had rubbed him with soap and bag,* they washed him and led him back to the dressing-room, covered with gold-wrought towels. After drying him gently, they decked his coarse sages' garb with a delicate shirt and elegant vestments, and perfumed him

* A small hair bag is used in baths for scrubbing the body.

with aloes-wood and ambergris, and, taking
him under the armpits, led him forth, saying,
" Come, our mistress awaits your happy
advent."

Poor Jewād, wondering in himself who
their mistress might be, accompanied the
slave-girls and came to a lofty pavilion, on
entering which, a darling of the world, a torment of the age, in the apparel of the
daughters of kings, advanced to welcome
him, saying, " Noble Jewād, you have
honoured me by your coming, and rejoiced
me." She took him by the hand and seated
him in the place of honour, and with caresses
and attentions gladdened his heart. A re-
fection was brought, and with a thousand
airs and charming graces they partook of
the delicious foods and drank of the delicate
wines ; and when bashfulness was turned
away and reserve cast off, that mistress of
the world threw her arms round Jewād's
neck, and, playing many a love-trick, they
rested till the evening in mirth and glee.
Then the world-adorning lady bade Jewād

good-night, and departed. They spread a
lofty couch for Jewād midmost the royal
pavilion, and dressed him in clean night-
clothes, and went away—they all dispersed
to slumber on the pillow of repose, leaving
Jewād alone.

Through his musing upon the circumstances of his case and on the beauty and
sweetness of that darling, sleep came not to
the eyes of Jewād till morning ; and behold,
when it was morning, the slave-girls came
and arrayed him in garments more splendid
than the former, and led him to another
room.   Now, the lady had awaited Jewād
since the dawn in the other room, to partake
of coffee along with him and to call him to
fresh delights ; so she saluted him with
" Good morning," and renewed were their
mirth and converse, and the party of glee.
In the portico of the pavilion, some twenty
slave-girls, musicians, playing upon full-
toned flute and viol, mandolin and rebeck,
made the world re-echo, and with the voices
of bejewelled singers and dancers it resounded;

and these delighted them. Then that world-
adorning darling asked for a lute, and, having
gracefully fitted the plectrum on her finger,
she screwed the peg of the lute and approached it to her crystal neck to hear how
it would sing, and passed her hand over it to
learn if it were the champion of the universe
of reproach* and the interpreter of the field
of art. Then she turned the sound into a
beauteous melody of the mode Hijāz,† and,
blending this in graceful cadence with the
modes Gerdāniyya† and Būselik,† she dis-
played such marvellous arts and such wondrous skill in the science of music, that she
inebriated and bewildered Jewād to that
degree that but one thread remained that he
brake not the chord and rent not the veil of
modesty.

When the noble maiden had thus shown
forth the art of playing and the art of en-
snaring, she returned the instrument to the

---

* Eastern music is of a sad and plaintive nature.

† These are names of modes in the Persian musical
system.

minstrel, and talking indifferently with
Jewād, again conversed with pleasant words
and graceful speeches.   They partook of a
collation, and when they were finished, their
conversation took the form of scientific and
philosophic discussion.   She was so versed
in science, and knowledge, and arts, and
philosophy, and exhibited such learning and
skill, that perfect amazement came over
Jewād.   Anon in mirth and glee and anon
in scientific converse they passed the time
till thus eleven days went by.   Then when
they again sat down to commune, the fair-
faced damsel, turning to Jewād, addressed
him thus, " My most noble lord, although by
reason of your being a sage and a philosopher, it is of your glory to be not precipitate
in any of your ways, yet, as a thousand
opportunities there-for have occurred in our
past conversations, your never having asked
who I am, is great patience and mighty self-
control."   Jewād replied, " My mistress, as
your lofty permission has been granted to
enquire, I crave that, deigning to lavish on

me your grace and your favour, you inform me regarding your sweet person, and instruct me concerning your fair self." So the maiden thus commenced her discourse: "This place is the city of Samarqand ; and your handmaid is Fitna-i Dil, the daughter of Gurshāsp Shāh, who now rules as monarch over this land. Since the days of childhood my desires have been restricted to the acquisition of knowledge, and they are grounded on the attainment of arts. Of all learning and sciences I have acquired some- what, according to my capability ; but especially do I incline to the arts of enchant- ment and talismans and magic and charms. My master, who is a learned elder named Khoja Bābek, the most wise of those in these parts, has left nought undone in teaching me what he knows of these sciences ; but as his skill in such arts falls short, I asked of him how I might gain the full knowledge thereof. He smiled and said, 'My daughter, in Antioch the Chief of the Sages, Ebū-'Alī Sīnā, has a spiritual son, Jewād by name, noble, high-

born, and distinguished by beauty. For all
he be not a prince, as that sage has taught
him all the sciences without exception that
he knows, he is a Pādishāh of the Seven
Climes, being possessed of such knowledge
as is worth the world. It is long since such
a fancy as this has occurred to my dreams
that it were more meet an accomplished
maiden like Your Felicitous Highness should
be married to such an one, a sovereign of the
hidden treasures of science and knowledge,
than to an unlearned prince. If you consent,
though it be not possible to fetch him with
the acquiescence of Ebū-'Alī, I your father,
will find a time when they think not, and
through my spiritual power bring him to
you.' Your handmaid became enamoured
of you, my lord, on hearing this ; and as my
father, the King, approved this matter and
gave his consent, I desired that my master
should transport you, my lord, in less than
a moment, to your lover's hovel. It was my
master Khoja Bābek who knocked at your
door. Dismiss disquiet from your noble

heart ; for *Praise God (exalted be He !)* your handmaid is pure and a virgin, otherwise I had not accepted my lord in marriage ; how could any man enter the harem of our chastity? Behold, my master, such is our case ; and at this moment this palace, this wealth, these riches, yea, the crown and throne of my feeble father belong to my lord ; your handmaid too is your lawful bride—but with this condition, that our dower and portion be not as those of others, but that you teach me beforehand, in lieu of dower, the Charm of Hārūt and Mārūt ; * and, in place of portion, the Phylacteria of Ahmed." †

Jewād, opening the mouth of excuse, said,‡ " It would seem that your teacher has been deceived in this matter by the false information of some person. Although I, your slave, am in the service of the noble Ebū-'Alī Sīnā,

* Two angels mentioned in the Qur'ān as being magicians.
† Certain kinds of amulets.
‡ The adepts were forbidden to communicate the mysteries to outsiders.

I am still a pupil engaged in such matters as
pounding with the mortar and weighing with
the scales ; I have never even heard the
names of the arts that you mention, or seen
the forms of the things that you describe."
She answered, " My Life, Jewād Chelebi, it
is unbecoming to act in this manner ; and,
think well and reflect, having once been ad-
mitted a confidant of the seclusion of our
private palace, how remote is escape!"
Although she entreated with caresses and
attentions, Jewād persisted in denying the
explanation ; so kindly love was turned to
rupture, and respect was changed to dis-
courtesy. The damsel knitted her gracious
brow, and the frown of anger appeared upon
her forehead ; and she said with fierceness,
" Alas! that deeming thee a man, we sought
to immerse thee in the ecstasy of union and
enrich thee with the vision of our beauty,
whilst thou art a low-bred wretch without
portion in the grace of favour ; respite is
granted thee for this night, gather thy senses
into thy head and reflect well ; for if on the

morrow thou still persist in this thy obstinacy
and deny those arts we ask of, death shall be
life to thee!" "Hence with this ill-omened
one!" she cried; and the slave-girls seized
poor Jewād by the collar, and shut him up
in a place like a vault. When Jewād entered
this prison he repeated magic charms and
performed what he knew of strange arts, but
as these availed him not one whit, and as no
sign appeared therefrom, dread overwhelmed
his heart, and he began to weep. He knew
that there was here some mighty power, for
that his magic incantations and performances
had no result; and he thought in himself,
with the finger of bewilderment in the
mouth,* "There must be some hidden reason
for this maiden's eager desire to learn certain
things of me while she herself is conversant
with arts that can render all my power of
none effect; this is fitting, that I yield up
my head but not my secret;" and he determined and resolved to part with life. He
wept till dawn in the narrow prison, and

* Biting the finger is considered a sign of perplexity.

when it was morn some of the eunuchs of
the harem opened the door and entered,
sword in hand. They made fast the hands
and feet of Jewād, and carried him before the
maiden, who, again adopting gentleness,
counselled and advised and promised him
much, and treated him with courtesy; but
after half an hour of this behaviour she
abandoned it, and threatened him for a like
space with frowns and wrath upon her brow.
She saw Jewād to be unbending in obstinacy,
that not only would he not reveal his secret,
but would not even seek refuge in pardon
and compassion; so she commanded the
eunuchs, saying, "Take this wretch and prepare his doom." So they seized him by the
neck and collar, and haled him to the mouth
of a pit; again she counselled him much,
but as not a sound proceeded from him save
the words of the Profession of Faith,* they
seized him by the feet, and cast him head
foremost down the pit.

* The Profession of Faith is: "*I testify that there is no god
but God, and I testify that Muhammed is the Apostle of God.*"

⁻As he descends headlong to the bottom of
the pit, he opens his eyes, and sees himself
sitting in the presence of Ebū-'Alī. For the
space of quarter of an hour he remained
speechless, overwhelmed in the ocean of
amaze. When he recovered his senses, he
kissed his master's feet, and manifested his
bewilderment, saying, " What has befallen
me ? " So his wise master thus addressed
him : " Son, we have caused thee a little
dismay ; but thou wilt hold us pardoned, for
this practice is of the honoured traditions of
the sages. From my perfect love for thee, I
did not much affright thee, but pitied thee.
Behold, my life, Jewād, this is a warning to
thee, and an example and a precedent to
conceal the Secrets.* They who conceal the
Secrets and yield up their lives shall find the
same in the presence of Glory, and likewise
the awakening from incertitude. I shall relate
to thee the strange experiences that my
master made me undergo to teach me the
concealment of the Secrets, that thou mayest

* The Secrets of Mystic Virtue.
B

know my gentleness and my tenderness towards thee."

THE STORY OF EBU-'ALI SINA.

"For thirty consecutive years, I, thy father, girded the loins of zeal and ardour in the service of my master, Khoja Dāhitī, in the city of Fez. One day, when I had to his satisfaction performed my duty and attained to that degree of knowledge to which thou, my son, hast reached, I went forth with the rest of the disciples to a field for diversion. As the students were numerous, pilaws and zerdas* were being cooked in cauldrons ; and, after the manner of amusement, the disciples played and entertained themselves with all sorts of games. One of the ushers showed us a game which consisted in tightly binding the eyes of one with a handkerchief; then that blindfolded one tried to catch one of the others, who teased him by plucking his hand and skirt ; when he caught one, his eyes were freed and

* The names of dishes.

those of the captive bound. By-and-by, the
blindfold lad caught me, and when they
were going to cover my eyes, our master said
jestingly, ' Ebū-'Alī is a cunning fellow ;
let me make fast his eyes.' And he
blindfolded me with the handkerchief himself, and led me into the middle of the field,
and there left me.   .

" I waited to catch my companions who
might come from either side, but no one appeared to pluck me. ' Come, now, do not
play any tricks when my eyes are thus
blindfolded,' cried I ; but no one came.
From the stress of my disquietude I tore the
handkerchief from my eyes, when what did I
see ? No longer the field where I had been
—I was standing in the midst of a boundless
waste. I said, ' *Glory to God ! There is no
strength nor any power saving in God !*'
And I sat down, and thinking to myself and
pondering, I remained bewildered. Finding
no help therefor, I arose and began to wander
vacantly over the plain. I fared on for the
space of five hours, when my strength and

endurance failed, but looking round about I saw upon a mound a saddled and caparisoned dromedary. I ascended the mound, and cautiously approaching the dromedary, I seized his bridle and mounted him. The moment I got upon him, he struck his feet upon the ground and soared into the air. What did I see? That which I rode was a hideous demon, and the bridle which I held in my hand was his elf-lock. Collecting my senses, I put into practice the charms which I had learned from my master; but when I perceived that these produced no effect soever, I began to weep.

"After flying in the air for the space of an hour, he alighted in a place like the Vale of Saqar.* There a vast multitude of demons, male and female, had lighted a great fire, and were gathered in a circle round about it; they had seized and bound a score of hapless ones of the sons of Adam, whom they stript to slaughter. The demon who had brought me took me down from his shoulder and

* The name of a stage of Hell.

placed me on the ground. Now, I gathered
from their gestures that the demons said on
seeing me, ' This lean man cannot be eaten
until he has been fattened for at least forty
or fifty days ; would that thou hadst not
brought him ! '—for I was thin of body and
meagre of person. And one by one they
came and looked at my hands and feet, and
they took me in their hands and examined
me like a sheep. At length they slaughtered
the men who were there, and thrust them
upon spits, and devoured them before my
eyes. Then they took me and imprisoned
me in a cave, and put beside me a measure
of walnuts and almonds and a pitcher of
water, and they made fast the cave door.

"Through my dismay I neither ate nor
drank, and half the night was passed when
sleep overcame me. I woke when it was
morning, and I found myself once more in
the waste. Praising and thanking God, I
wandered along the plain, and while casting
my eyes distractedly around lest a wild man
might appear, I perceived a frail old man

proceeding along the road straight before
me. On my approaching and saluting him,
he said, 'Why dost thou wander in this
place?' And I related to him all my adventures of the day before. He said : 'O,
my son, God hath indeed protected thee ;
these are a set of demons such that escape is
impossible for those who fall into their
hands ; our being able to pass through these
parts is only by virtue of our knowledge of
the Most Great Name. Do not fear, thy
meeting with us is owing to the prayers of
thy master ; come, be a guest in our house ;
our village is hard by.'

" We fared along together for about three
hours, and while on the road he said a
thousand pleasant things. When we entered
the village the old man shook himself once,
and his stature grew to the height of twenty
cubits, and he uttered a yell, like the roar of
a cannon, which well-nigh broke the mem-
branes of my ear ; and immediately were
gathered together four or five hundred
creatures hideous like himself. When I

beheld this I commenced to repeat charms,
and again I saw that these magic rites had
no effect, so I remained helpless and bewildered. Amongst the demons was a form
more vile than all the rest, clad in the garb
of a woman ; now this was the daughter of
the accursed one who had brought me. He
made me over to her, saying, 'Take this
wretch and fulfil thy duty ; he has wearied
me much upon the road.' Then she seized
me by the arm, and put me into a dark cave,
and sat down beside me, and said, 'Stranger,
do not fear ; my father gave thee to me that
he might eat thee ; but I have fallen in love
with thee. All the demons are ravished with
my beauty ; thou seest how fair I am ; although the fear of death at present bewilders
thee, I doubt not that on the first glance
thou too shalt love my beauty and grace and
comeliness. My will is to rejoice thee with
the delight of union with me ; but in matters
like this there must be no precipitation ; see,
for some days let us talk and converse with
one another, then thou shalt be mine, and I

will be thine.' She brought me a tin dish in
which was a roasted· dog, and a pitcher of
water, and said, 'Now, my darling, eat,
drink, and be at ease ;' and she departed. I
sought refuge in God and repented me of
my past sins, and through despair and fatigue,
wept passing sore.

"When it was morning I awoke and
opened my eyes, and, lo, I was near a city.
Thanking and praising God for the separation from my lover, I arose and proceeded
towards the city. On the way I encountered
both on hill and plain many animals, such
as horses and asses and apes and dogs ;
these gathered round me and pulled me by
·the hand and skirt, and with their mute
eloquence would have hindered me from
going into the city ; but I repelled them and
entered it. When I passed into the city I
saw standing ready prepared a fresh and
regal horse, with some twenty or thirty servants ; these, saying, 'Welcome, my master!'
mounted me on the steed, and, following at
my stirrup, conducted me to an imperial

palace. I saw the city to be very flourishing, and the palace exceeding splendid and magnificent, and I marvelled. They conducted me with respect to the royal divan ; and all the members of the divan were standing, and a veiled monarch was sitting upon a throne on the chief place of a dais. So I went to the foot of the throne and kissed the ground and modestly retired, whereupon the sovereign asked me whence I came. On my narrating how I had by enchantment fallen into a wilderness, and the adventures I had encountered during the two nights, the monarch smiled wonderingly, and said, ' Thou hast met with marvellous haps,' and he bade fetch a chair and motioned me to be seated. When the business of the divan was finished, permission was granted to every one, and they went away. Presently an officer came and took me, and bringing me before the palace-gate, made me over to the harem eunuchs, who conducted me with the greatest deference. On entering a vast pavilion I saw upon a throne a darling

of the world, a torment of the soul, the
description of whose charms would surpass
that of Fitna-i Dil's by a hundred degrees.
She said, ' All hail! come hither.' And she
took me to her side and, after a thousand
caresses and attentions, looked upon me and
addressed me thus, ' Ebū-'Alī, speak truly,
hast thou ever in the course of thy life seen
ór heard of a darling of the world equal to
me ?' I replied, '*I seek pardon of God*, my
mistress, the truth is, that the like of thy
world-adorning beauty exists not on the
earth, nor has been heard of.' Then she said,
' O Ebū-'Alī, this city is the city of Sūrat,
and the realm which is under my sway ; for
I am Shīrīn-Kār, sovereign of the land of
Sūrat. I inherited this realm from my
father, and for five years have I sat without
misfortune on my paternal throne. I am
the monarch whom a little while ago thou
sawest covered with a veil, sitting on the
throne. As the neighbouring monarchs
round about are lords of might, resistance
would be difficult, did they make war upon

us. Alike my father and your handmaid
have been able to rule this country only
through the spiritual power of my nurse
Ruveyda ; but knowing not what would be-
fall me if to that nurse there happened a
mischance, I took counsel with her upon this
matter, and she gave answer thus : " My
daughter, there is in Fez a darling disciple of
Khoja Dāhitī, who possesses much skill in
the science of magic, and his science is more
potent than our enchantments. I shall bring
him to thee, for he is full worthy to be thy
mate ; and thou shouldst wed him, and
relinquishing crown and throne, rest in the
corner of retirement." I said, "If Ebū-'Alī
possess such magic power, how can I be
safe with him ? Should he be vexed with
me, peradventure he might seek to injure
me." My nurse replied, " There is a remedy
for this too ; let Ebū-'Alī teach thee the
Hintij Charm, which is the most potent of
all magic charms, and henceforward he will
be powerless to harm us." Thus we decided ;
and she went and snatched thee from the

field. That dromedary which thou sawest
and which afterwards became a demon, and
that aged man thou didst meet the next
day were our old nurse. And each of these
animals thou sawest without the city is a
skilful magician whom my nurse has trans-
formed and driven to the wilds for seeking
to overcome us. In a word, my object in
briefly relating these things to thee—and
delay and deliberation are needless in this
matter—is that in an hour's time thou
teachest that charm to thy handmaid ; and
one day our wedding shall surely be.' Now,
as the charm she spoke of was the formula
which I had several times repeated both on
the demon's back and in the negress's cave,
and from which I had seen no result, I was
doubly astonished, and remained silent.
Perceiving from my silence my resolution
not to comply, she urged me the more ; and
at length when she saw that I absolutely re-
fused, she showed forth her anger, and said
to frighten me, 'Delay not, or I will slay
thee.' When she saw it to be altogether

vain, she summoned the executioner, and
made me over to him, saying, 'Finish the
work for me.' So he bound my hands with
a handkerchief and made me kneel down,
and as I was looking for death, someone
brushed against my sleeve. Fancying it to
be the executioner, I was about to cry for
quarter, when all the disciples shouted out,
'He has caught him!' They did off the
bandage from my eyes, and I saw I was
again in the playground in the field. My
master came up to me and said, 'Ebū-'Alī's
stomach is disordered, his head is reeling.'
And he took me by the hand and made me
sit down beside him, and whispered in my
ear, 'Fear not.' And he said to one of the
ushers, 'Ebū-'Alī has fasted for three days,
bring the pilaw quickly.' Silent and bewildered I ate of the pilaw and zerda with
the disciples ; and when evening was nigh,
after we had returned from the field to our
old abode, my master no longer concealed
from me the knowledge of the arcana—*the
mercy of God on him !*" *

* These experiences of Jewād and Ebū-'Alī are suggestive

"Behold! Jewād, Light of my eyes, be it
known unto thee and believed that of such
strange sciences one is Sorcery (Sihr), to
perform which—*refuge is in God (exalted be
He!)*—is degradation to our nature and contrary to the Divine pleasure ; it is an ever-
increasing sin dependent on the uttering of
vile words blaspheming the Eternal Glory,
and connected with abominable acts. There
is another which consists of marvels brought
about by the means of certain names of
Spiritual Beings, and virtues of things, and
charms ; this they call Magic (Sīmyā).
Another, connected with the influences of the
stars, they name the Science of Talismans
(Tilsim) or Enchantments (Nīrenjāt). Another, too, is effected by seclusion and vigils
and fasts and austerities, with certain Qur-
'ānic verses and Divine names and charms ;
this is called the Science of Occult Virtues
('Ilm-i Khawāss). There is yet another

of the effects of some of the intoxicating preparations, such
as bang or hashish, employed in the East. It is probable
that the magicians made frequent use of such.

kind, the Divine Science, the Celestial Knowledge ; this traversing of time and space
which thou hast witnessed is only effected by
that glorious Science, those Divine Mysteries.
Be it not concealed that the Lords of Truth
and the Companions of the Grace of Knowledge have ascertained that the faculty of
imagination exerciseth power in twenty-
seven matters. For example, if a pure man
conversant with the Divine Subtleties conceive in his mind the perfect likeness of
the external form of any person, mould an
image thereof, and keep the same in some
narrow place, like a cupboard, it is well
known that he whose image is thus formed,
wheresoever he be, will fall a prey to contraction of breast and heaviness of heart. In
like manner the accomplishment of such
traversing of space and time is of the powers
of the understanding. For this cause were
the magic charms that thou knowest of no
effect, and wast thou unable to release thyself from the trammels of the prison—that
the Divine Knowledge is more potent than

all other sciences. Moreover, be it believed
of thee that what thou sawest were not mere
visions, and that we instructed Fitna-i Dil to
observe such conduct toward thee. In
short, these things which thou didst behold
are all at this moment in existence ; and, an
it be thy desire, I will wed thee to that
darling maiden. But I crave of thee,
Endowed with Knowledge, ever to move
about a celibate, and that thou violate not
the custom of the sages :—to be in the world,
like Saint Jesus, without a spouse. In truth,
my object in the cruel treatment shown to
thee by that maiden was to induce thee to
shun them, having seen the fickleness of women."

Ebū-'Alī, after confirming, as requisite,
pledge and troth with Jewād, said, " O son,
thou hast gained a manifest right henceforward to acquire the Blessed Knowledge—
may it be blessed to thee ! " And breast to
breast he explained and conveyed to Jewād
all that he knew of the Divine Science. So
Jewād became a greater master than his

master in mystic and philosophic lore, and in the general and special sciences a wonder working sage.

When seven years had thus passed, total feebleness came over Ebū-'Alī's human elements by reason of the greatness of his age ; and, as the journey to the Hereafter became inevitable, he called all his disciples round his bed, and, after making the necessary testaments, he appointed Jewād his successor, and closed his lips repeating the best of finishings, the words of the Profession of Faith, and set forth for Paradise.

After the consignment to the sepulchre, whilst the rites of mourning were being fulfilled and completed, Jewād was not negligent of teaching and instructing, but busied in the diffusion of knowledge. But as he was still in the years of his youth, the old ushers could not endure that he should sit on the carpet of master ; and, seeing that they vexed him by ridicule and derision, he was obliged to leave that district ; and he set out alone for the city of Constantinople. When he reached

c

the capital he thus said in himself, 'If I go
to the colleges where are the learned, my
time will again be occupied in instructing
and instruction, and I shall assuredly gain
no pleasure by reason of the conduct of the
vulgar ; a better joy were to conceal my
power and skill, and going amongst the
people, endeavour to promote their happiness.'
So he hired a room in the Armour-Bearer's
Khan and remained in the corner of retirement, occupying himself in visiting the places
worthy to be seen in the streets and markets
of the Sublime Capital.

One day, as he was going up from the Long
Bazaar, he saw some dozen of witty-look-
ing friends gathered together in the shop of
a respectable person who sold cups and soap
and certain drugs, opposite the shop of
'Ushshāqī-Oghlu ; these invited him to come
in and enjoy himself. Saying in himself,
'If they be of the Sublime Capital, they
will be an intelligent set,' he saluted them
in an easy manner, and got into the shop.
The shopkeeper, who was a person named

Ibrāhīm Chelebi, and one of the polished men of the day, treated Jewād courteously, saying, 'Welcome! all hail!' and he regaled him with coffee and tobacco. Jewād paid attention to the converse of the friends, and when he saw that they were all select, agreeable, sweet of speech, clever and witty, he joined in the conversation on fitting opportunities, so that all the friends were delighted at his words, and asked whence he came and where he dwelt ; and the shopkeeper and the comrades sang his praises, requesting he would always rejoice them by coming.

So Jewād, who loved such gatherings of intelligent friends, began to go regularly to that place, and bound the bonds of friendship and familiarity with all the comrades, but especially with the shopkeeper Ibrāhīm Chelebi the soap-merchant, to such a degree that if any day he came not, it was because he was indisposed ; and Ibrāhīm's eyes would be fixed upon the road, and that day he would not smile.

In the still existing and famous shop of

'Ushshāqī-Oghlu, which was opposite, was
then a youth, a darling of the world, a dis-
turber of the age, of the House of 'Ushshāqī, about sixteen or seventeen years old,
called Monla Emīn, who sometimes came
to the shop of Ibrāhīm Chelebi to have
private conversations. One day Jewād said
to Ibrāhīm Chelebi, ' This son of ' Ushshāqī
sometimes comes and sits here, but never
joins in the conversation ; I had imagined
him vain of his comeliness, but on looking
with attention I see that he always sits in
his own shop too, sad and sorrowful ; here
the signs of grief and distress seem still
greater.'   Ibrāhīm Chelebi shook his head
and said, ' My master, a strange adventure
has befallen him, a circumstance the like of
which has not been seen or heard.'   And
thus began he to relate :—

THE STORY OF MONLA EMIN.

"Mustejeb Chelebi, the father of this young
man, died a year ago, and left his shop, his
house, with some other things and about a

hundred purses,* which the latter inherited.
I had formerly relations with his father, and
as Emīn was quite young, fearing that he
might go astray, I urged him to marry. The
lad disputed not my words, but consented ;
so sending examiners† round, we began to
look for a bride for Monla Emīn. One day
the old women came and reported that near
the Varigated Bath, there was a damsel,
daughter of a person named Hājī Mustafa
the slipper-seller. She had inherited from
her late father, besides a house and much
garniture, a monthly income of two hundred
and fifty piastres, the rent of some property.
She had no friends but her mother, and was
now sixteen or seventeen years old ; and no
words could describe her beauty, which was
worth the world : a lovely maiden, black-
eyebrowed, blue-eyed, with skin whiter than
whiteness, with figure and stature well-
proportioned, with long neck, with hands,

* A " purse " consists of 500 piastres.
† The old women mentioned in the next sentence.

feet, and mouth all to match, with cheek and
forehead like the moon, in airs and graces a
torment of the world, an ensnarer, a heart-
delighter, a cause of joy.   And they stated
how when they declared that the seeker in
marriage was Monla Emīn, her mother consented, saying, 'Monla Emīn shall be an
indoor bridegroom (that is he shall come to
the maiden's house and we will see to the
daily expenses, nothing shall be looked for
from him) ; I only want a well-mannered
son-in-law, one who will open and shut our
doors, and such like.'   Much pleased at this
news, I informed Monla Emīn, who consented
and appointed your slave agent ; and two of
the companions being the witnesses, we
married ' Ayesha, daughter of Mustafa, to
Mehemed Emīn Agha ; and in the course of
a few days their union was consummated.
For about a month they got on somehow, for
although Monla Emīn was satisfied with his
wife, his mother-in-law was such a cruel,
wicked, unmannerly wretch, that there was
not a day but she sent him weeping to the

shop. When I saw this state of things, and that the poor young man's health and happiness were banished, at my instance his wife was divorced.

" Some twenty days after this event, a well-dressed, well-fashioned and handsome man of about sixty-five years of age, attended by four servants, happening to pass by, saw the cases of drugs displayed in my shop. He dismounted and came into my poor shop, and after saluting me politely, asked, ' Master, have you benzoin and crocus martis ?' Answering, 'Yes,' I placed these drugs before him. He separated five drachms of each, and, paying the money, put each into a piece of paper, and taking a bit of muslin from his bosom, placed them in it. That man was so eloquent and polite that both your slave and the friends were delighted with his tone and manners ; but he bade us farewell, and mounted his horse again and departed. In the course of ten days he happened to pass by here, and he alighted and, coming into the shop, said, ' Ibrāhīm Chelebi, by

Allah I was greatly pleased with thee.' He
was very courteous, and your slave treated
him with marked attention ; and he tarried
for about three hours, and then went away.
He continued coming at intervals of a few
days, and grew familiar with us ; and in the
space of a month he came twenty times to
our shop. He mentioned at a fitting time
in the course of conversation that he was of
the Chartered Fief-Holders and that his
name was 'Abbās Agha. Our Monla Emīn
too was present now and then at the meetings. One day I related Emīn's adventure
to the Agha, just as I have told it to you ;
he showed much regret, and finding a break
in the conversation, said, ' My dear Ibrāhīm
Chelebi, I pray that to-morrow you honour
my poor house with a visit, and bring Monla
Emīn ; you might have some difficulty in
finding the house, so I will send a servant to
you.' I replied, ' I shall be honoured and
delighted.' So at three o'clock next day he
sent a servant with two horses with Hayderī
bridles and saddle-cloths of Mārdīn work.

We mounted the horses and followed the
servant till we came to a large door in a
blind-alley near the Cap-maker's Mosque in
the New Garden. When we entered the
court some thirty, tidy, well-dressed pages,
with sashes round their waists, came forward
to the horse-block to meet us, and taking
hold of our skirts, they respectfully led us
up-stairs. It was a palace in size nearly
equal to the residence of the Grand Vezir ;
we entered a room spread with carpets such
as are not to be found in the dwellings of the
greatest of the great. His Excellency the
Agha with a black-fox pelisse on his vezirial
shoulders, was seated in a corner, and a
similar number of chosen pages were standing before him with folded hands; and I was
amazed at the pomp and magnificence of
the Agha. When he saw us he rose and
said, ' O brothers, you have wearied your
feet ; you have done me honour.' And he
treated us with courtesy, and we kissed his
skirt and sat down. A collation was served,
and after it had been partaken of, the Agha

arose and went into a small room adjoining
the other ; then a page appeared and said to
me, ' Pray come, the Agha wishes you.'
And he took me and brought me into his
presence. As he motioned me to sit near
him, I sat down facing him, knee to knee,
and he said, 'Ibrāhīm Chelebi, I am about to
make a request of thee, and I desire of
thee that thou do gratify it ; what sayest
thou ?' I replied, ' How could I refuse anything I can perform ?' Then he said, ' In
this mansion, the world, I have no heir save
one only daughter ; my desire is to make
Monla Emīn my son-in-law ; but I wish that
he be persuaded now, for I desire to make
this day the wedding-day and this night the
bridal-night ; if thou say ' nay,' it will be
needful to sever the thread of friendship.'
I replied, 'Lo, my master, I shall go and explain to him.' And I arose and came to
him. On my informing him of what had
passed, he said, ' Thou art my father, whatsoever thou do I approve.' So I went to the
Agha and told him that Emīn consented.

He immediately sent men to the imām* and
assembly of the parish, and we returned to
the first room. Emīn kissed the Agha's
skirt and blessed him saying, ' Be happy,'
and while conversing about how they would
get on and such like, the imām and Remzī
Chelebi, the mu'ezzin† of the mosque, who
was an old friend of ours, and other people
of the parish came and seated themselves
politely. Remzī Chelebi sat down beside
me, bowed to me, and said, ' It is long since
we have seen each other.'   On my explaining
to him in a low voice the reason of his being
summoned and what was wanted of the
party, he said : ' *What things God willeth,
exalted be He !* May He grant peace and
happiness !   Emīn has attained to fortune,
when not so much as looking for it.'
The pipes were now removed, and while
censers of aloes-wood and ambergris were
smoking, the Imām Efendi, vowing repentance and begging forgiveness, recited

* Precentor.   † Caller to Divine Service.

an eloquent marriage-service, and wedded
Khayāl Khānim, daughter of 'Abbās Agha,
to Mehemed Emīn, with a paid-down dower
of one thousand piastres. A grey-squirrel
pelisse with ample sleeves was given to the
Imām Efendi, bags of money to Remzī
Chelebi and the two other mu'ezzins, and,
according to the usual custom, muslin hand-
kerchiefs to the party ; beside me, too, they
laid a parcel. After the completion of the
ceremony, the Agha said, ' I hope, *if it please
God*, you will also perform the evening-
worship here ? ' Leave was then given to
every one, and they departed. When we
were left alone the Agha said, ' Let us send
Emīn Agha to the bath.' So we sent him
to the bath mounted on a caparisoned horse
accompanied by two attendants. Your slave
also took leave of His Excellency the Agha,
and went to shut the shop, having agreed to
come back early on the morrow, if it pleased
God. So I closed the shop and went to my
house, and praised God for the parcel that
had been given me, and thanked Him for

THE STORY OF JEWAD.

Emīn's attaining this unlooked-for good fortune.

" When it was morning I went and opened my shop and got a hired horse, and while I was waiting wondering if it were time to go to Monla Emīn's father-in-law, a halberdier* came up, and, saluting me, asked, 'Who is Ibrāhīm Chelebi the soap-merchant here?' On my telling him that I was he, he said, ' Pray come ; some one whom the bastinado-men have wants you, and begs that you come quickly.' As the horse was ready, I mounted and went to the Hôtel, when what did I see? —it was Monla Emīn who was in the prison. My soul leapt into my head, and I asked, ' What is this plight?' Then he said : ' O my good father, I have met with a strange adventure, the like of which has never happened to anyone. At the time when they took me to the bath, after the cleansing, they

* A Janissary employed as an official messenger.

† The Hôtel or Palace, the official residence of the Agha of the Janissaries.

arrayed me in these splendid garments I
have on, and put into my pocket four hundred half sequins* for the expenses of the
bath—the rest are in my pocket still. They
took me from the bath and brought me to
the mansion ; and after supper, when it was
evening, the Imām and the Mu'ezzin Remzī
Chelebi and the assembly returned and performed the ceremony of evening-worship ;
and they put me into the bridal-chamber. I
had imagined to myself, 'As I am chosen
son-in-law of a distinguished person like this,
his daughter must be vile and foul of favour,
degraded in the eyes of the great, or smitten
with some illness ; but for the sake of this
fortune, let it be what it will.' But when I
entered the nuptial apartment (I cannot
describe the splendours of the bridal-chamber) what did I see ? That she was a bride
the like of whom in beauty and loveliness
and grace and comeliness had never entered
the imagination or conception of that son-

* A sequin was worth about 12s. 6d.

in-law, the aged Sphere.   It was after six
o'clock when sleep overcame me.   When it
was morning I awoke, but finding not my
beloved in the bed, I rose up, and what did I
see ?—that darling of the world lying mur-
dered in the middle of the room, with her
head and hands and feet separated, in ten
pieces.   O my dear, my good father ! that
moment my breath was stopped; I fell down
fainting.   After a time my senses returned,
and weeping, I went out of the room.   The
nurse and slave-girls, who were waiting without the door, said, ' What is the matter ? '
I replied, 'Go in and see what is the matter.'
Then when the nurse went in and saw the
bride in that case, her cries and wails, like
the voice of a Mu'ezzin, ascended to Capella ;
and all the slave-girls gathered together and
wailed aloud.   And they informed my father-
in-law, and he came, and when he saw his
daughter in such case, he fell down in a
swoon.   They sprinkled water upon his face
and brought back his senses ; and he rushed
upon me crying, ' O wretch ! O fool ! is this

the return for the favours I conferred upon
thee ?   O traitor !'   Then he fetched his
servants and other retainers, and showed
them what had happened, and said, ' Take
this wretch to the Agha of the Janissaries
and explain what has occurred ; I, too, shall
go when she who is slain has been washed
and buried.'   And he gave me to three of
his servants, who, dragging me by hand and
collar, brought me here ; and when they had
informed the Agha, he imprisoned me in this
place.'   Crying, ' Ah ! my good father, do
this with my shop and that with my money,'
Emīn made his testament, and began to shed
tears like rain by reason of the fire within
his heart.   To comfort him, I said, ' Fear
not ; *God is good !*'   But he made answer :
' How should I fear ?   Thou fanciest that I
weep through dread of death ; after parting
from a fairy-faced bride like her, to die were
life to my soul.   Would to God that I had
died an hour before her, that I might have
met her in the Hereafter !   I weep for part-

ing from my love.' And he wept full bitterly, so that my heart was pierced.

" I thought much within myself and thus decided—that there was no help save to go once more to 'Abbās Agha and tell him of the anguish of poor Emīn, that perchance he might forgive him. With this purpose I mounted upon my beast, and with fear and trembling turned into the blind-alley near the mosque in the New Garden. But I could find no door like the great gate I had seen the night before ; and while I was standing in the middle of the street in perfect bewilderment, an old woman called from behind a lattice, 'What seekest thou, son ? ' On my answering, 'There is here one of the chartered fief-holders, 'Abbās Agha ; I am seeking his mansion,' she replied, ' There is no such person or mansion as you mention here.' I left the street, and knocking at some doors, asked the same question. When I could get no information, I recollected that Remzī Chelebi had been there the night before ; so thinking to go and enquire of him, I went

D

and found him. 'Ah! welcome,' said he;
'what wind has blown you here?' I replied,
'O brother, I am seeking that house of
'Abbās Agha where we were last night at
the marriage of Monla Emīn; I cannot find
it; would you do me the kindness to show
it to me?' Then Remzī Chelebi's gaiety
disappeared, and he answered: 'Ibrāhīm
Chelebi, what has happened to thee? What
'Abbās Agha? What marriage? It is a
year since I have seen thee; what ails thee?'
I replied, 'O brother, thou didst sit by my
side last evening, and thou didst ask me so-
and-so, and I answered thee on such an wise.'
'Alas, alas, brother,' said he, 'do not delay
in getting thyself bled and in taking a strong
draught.' I then knew there was some
mystery here, and I said, 'Do not think,
brother, Remzī Chelebi, that I am afflicted
with melancholia; listen to my words.' And
I related to him the whole story. I said,
'And Monla Emīn is now in prison; for the
love of God come with me to the Hôtel and
see.' And I took Remzī Chelebi to the

Hôtel of the Agha. When he saw Emīn in prison and asked the truth of him, and he related the entire adventure, Remzī Chelebi, unable to comprehend, cried, ' *Glory to God! there is no strength nor any power saving in God!* O my son, it is a year since I have seen thee or Ibrāhīm Chelebi.' And he became more bewildered than ourselves.

"Then we both went up together to the presence of the Agha and related to him all that had happened, and Remzī said : ' My master, I, your slave, am the Mu'ezzin of that parish ; and there is no such man in our parish ; and, whilst I have not seen these two men for a year, they insist that we spoke to each other last night : there is here some strange mystery ; investigate and look into it.' The Agha said : ' Yes, the slaves too who brought the murderer in the morning stated that their master was a fief-holder named 'Abbās Agha, who resided near the Cap-maker's Mosque.' And he sent one man to the New Garden and another to enquire of the Chief of the Fief-holders. When these

returned, the first reported that there was no
such person in that quarter, and the second
that the Chief of the Fief-holders could find
in his register no fief-holder of that name
who resided in the capital. So the Agha
was plunged in the ocean of amazement, and
with the security of us two he liberated Emīn
from prison and gave him over to us. We
took him to the shop, but what was the use?
—his eyes would not look upon the world,
and he would say nothing but, 'Why did
you save me ; and not leave me that they
might have killed me, then I should have
met my darling a little sooner in the Hereafter?' We then took him by force to his
shop, opened it, and seated him in his place.
We perceived a piece of paper, of the size of
a ticket, lying on the counter ; and thus was
there written thereon :—'Filthy swine, nor
has 'Abbās Agha any being, nor has the
damsel any existence ; it is I, thy mother-in-
law, who have done all this ; I will teach
thee to abandon my daughter for a few words
of mine ; this thing is the least that I will

do ; see, will it suffice thee ? ' When we
read the paper we were still more bewildered ;
and by reason of the greatness of our fear we
again sent an agent and caused Emīn to
renew the marriage with his divorced wife.
He is therefore now compelled to endure
suffering, and the grief thereof is the cause of
his sadness."

Jewād smiled and said, ' Ibrāhīm Chelebi,
if you have a quiet place I will show you
a strange sight.' Ibrāhīm replied, ' There
cannot be a quieter place than Monla Emīn's
own house in the neighbourhood of Merjān.'
So Monla Emīn and Ibrāhīm Chelebi and
Jewād went all three to that house, and
entering, locked the door and sat down in a
room. Then Jewād addressed Monla Emīn,
saying, ' Get ready a complete suit of clothes
of thine own garments, and a piece of myrtle,
or laurel, or olive, or pomegranate-wood a
span long, and bring them.' So he went,
and according to the directions brought the
clothes and a piece of myrtle-wood ; then

Jewād cut the wood with a knife to the thickness of a reed-pen, making it four-sided, and said, '*And this is the wand of Tabātib, take it with the hand of El-Qaytarā.*'* And he gave it into the hand of Emīn, and thus directed him: 'Do thou go now to thy house, and while talking with thy wife, do thou strike her once with that wand, as it were in play; and do thou come to the shop and recount to us whatsoever thou mayest have beheld. But let us make trial here : strike thyself once with it, and let us see.' The moment Emīn struck himself with the wand all his clothes vanished, and he stood naked as when he came from his mother. At once he got the clothes he had made ready and put them on ; and he and Ibrāhīm Chelebi were amazed at this occurrence. Then Jewād said, 'Monla Emīn, brother, those clothes which thou hadst on were magical unrealities ; from the day when first I beheld

* I have been unable to ascertain who or what Tabātib and El-Qaytarā are.

thee I have seen thee naked ; now go and
strike once thy wife in compliance with my
instructions, and we shall see.'   So he sent
Emīn to his wife's house, and went with
Ibrāhīm Chelebi to the shop.   In the course
of half-an-hour Emīn arrived smiling and
delighted, and he kissed the hand of Jewād.
And the latter said, ' Restore the trust,' and
he took the wand and brake it.   Then he
asked, saying, ' Now let us see, what hast
thou done ?'   And Emīn thus narrated :
' When I got to the house I entered my
usual room and sat down, and my wife said
to me, ' My life, what has happened that thou
comest thus untimely ?'   I gave no answer,
but struck her once with the wand, and that
very moment that peerless beauty turned
into a ragged hag, like an eighty-year-old,
two-humped, toothless, gipsy sieve-seller ;
and that house like a lofty mansion became
a vile and filthy one-roomed old hovel ; and
that sumptuous garniture was changed into
a tattered government-store rug and two
canvas bolsters stuffed with straw.   The

woman began to weep and cry, ' Mercy ! for
the love of God destroy me not !' ' Who art
thou, speak the truth?' said I. She answered,
' They call me Bloody 'Ayesha, and she
whom thou imaginest to be thy mother-in-
law is my younger sister.' ' Swear to me,'
said I, ' that thou wilt never again bewitch
me or come before me, else will I strike thee
again and slay thee.' And I made her swear
strong oaths, and left her, and am come.'
And Ibrāhīm Chelebi smiled and was
delighted, and blessed Jewād ; and he prepared musked coffee, and the three of them
enjoyed themselves once more alone in the
shop. In the course of conversation Jewād
said to Ibrāhīm, ' My dear Ibrāhīm Chelebi,
have we finished our business yet ? We
have left Monla Emīn wifeless ; it were right
that we should make him again head of a
house.' But poor Emīn, as his wool had
been singed twice already, cried out, 'Mercy,
my master, henceforward marriage is unlawful for me ; you have delivered me, that is
sufficient kindness.'

Once, after about ten days had passed in
this fashion, when they were wearied with the
greatness of the heat of the weather, Jewād
said to Ibrāhīm, 'My life, Ibrāhīm Chelebi,
the heart longs for some shady retreat ; the
walks about Hayder Pasha* are said to be
beautiful, what if you and Monla Emīn and
I were all three to go a-pleasuring there ?'
' My master,' replied Ibrāhīm, ' God knows
you have spoken well; your slave too was
imagining how delightful it would be. *If it
please God (exalted be He !)* after to-morrow,
which is Friday and the holiday of all the
folk at Hayder Pasha, your slave and Monla
Emīn will get ready some eatables.'   Said
Jewād, ' My lord, there is no need for you to
trouble ; I, your slave, have one or two
domestics who prepare exceeding delicious
dishes ; I shall take them and go over first.
If at two o'clock you and Monla Emīn get
into a boat and come across, you will find

* A suburb of Constantinople on the Asiatic side of the
Sea of Marmara.

your slave in the Chief Florist's Garden.'
And they agreed thereto.

On the appointed day at two o'clock, as
had been arranged, Ibrāhīm Chelebi and
Monla Emīn got into a boat and passed over
to Hayder Pasha. What did they see ?—in
the Chief Florist's Garden was a regal
parade. They wondered where Jewād could
be, and just as they were going to search
for him, a handsome, well-dressed page, with
some servants, came up to them, and approaching Ibrāhīm Chelebi, saluted him, and
said, 'Our master has seen your arrival with
a spy-glass, and he desires you.' Poor
Ibrāhīm Chelebi and Emīn could not think
what had befallen them, and when with fear
and trembling they entered the Garden, many
pages came forward to salute them, and they
brought them before a magnificent tent
formed of a single piece of gold brocade ;
and they saw that the Pādishāh of the Age
who sat therein clad in lovely raiment was
Jewād. When Jewād saw Ibrāhīm Chelebi
he laughed aloud and said, 'Come, brothers,

it seems you have been searching for us much.' They could not utter a word, and bewildered, were about to kiss his skirt, but he hindered them saying, '*I seek pardon of God*, brothers, our wish is not to overpower you; but I thought, 'What diversion were there in a poor stroll? Let us have a kingly spectacle.' If you love God, change not your manner; and if you are afraid we shall leave this pageantry and go alone beneath the trees; come then, my lords.' And he took his companions and seated them by his side. After coffee had been partaken of in regal style, he said, 'Come, let us go up.' And with serjeants bearing Chinese bells* marching along side of them and crying to the people to form in order, and with pages respectfully leading them, they ascended in pomp to an elevated saloon like unto the vault of heaven. All the attendants in that palace were rosy-cheeked damsels; these met

* The military musical instrument called in French *chapeau chinois*. The Turkish name is *chevgān*; none of the dictionaries give this meaning of that word.

them at the head of the steps with jewelled
censers, and respectfully conducted them to
a lofty pavilion, the walls and doors whereof
were like the lustres called 'jewelled musks,'
which women fasten on their heads. The
description of the garniture of a pavilion of
which the very walls were begemmed is
needless. About five hundred slave-girls,
beautiful, distracters of the world, stood ready
to serve ; some of them were attired in the
usual garb of women ; others in trousers,
waistcoat, jacket, and small fez, with coiled
top-knot ; others again in petticoats like
Frankish women ; and others like sailors,
Greek islanders, and seraglio pages with
turbaned cap and girdled waist. The friends
sat down in the place of honour in the
pavilion, round a jewel-set golden tray,
whereon were spread, like a Ramazān breakfast, a thousand unknown and unheard of
conserves and fruits and other things, such as
salads and Candian curds. After partaking
of many strange and wonderful delicacies and
luxuries, flavoured with attar and ambergris

and musk,—things which had never entered
into the mind of the cook, the Sphere,—they
washed their hands in a basin made of
a single emerald, the ewer of which was of a
single ruby, and when they had wiped them
with embroidered towels of silk of Esterābād,
they went into a room whereof the doors and
walls were of carved and graven aloes-wood
of Māverd, gold-embossed, and the windows
of crystal-like diamond, and the cushions and
carpets of the embroidery of Lahore and
Cashmere, one in hue. Some two hundred
slave-girls clad in splendid garments in shade
like the garniture stood ready to serve.
Coffee and pipes were brought ; and after
thirty slave-girl musicians, singers and dancers, had appeared and entertained them by
their arts, they commenced to converse, and
Jewād thus addressed Ibrāhīm Chelebi, ' O,
my lord, I know that you now think these
things which you behold to be like the magic
enchantments of Bloody 'Ayesha, and that
your heart is no longer troubled ; but be it
known unto you that not only this which

you see, but worlds as they actually exist
(many times more strange and marvellous
than this), which may not be conceived or
imagined, are gifts from the Creator to the
Adepts.   Through the power of God *(exalted
be He !)* repose is granted to our wishes in
these worlds during what time we desire.
These things are not sorcery, or magic, or
spells, or enchantment, or delusions ; keep
your mind at rest, be not dismayed.   The
cause of your having seen this world, and of
your virtues, is but the favour of the Lord
Most High towards you.   Well, now, Monla
Emīn, my wish is to marry thee ; *if it please
God (exalted be He !)* thou shalt forget the
sorrows thou hast endured.'

'Call a messenger,' cried Jewād to the
slave-girls ; and immediately there entered
a dwarf, hairy and bearded, with propor-
tionate hands and feet, and a cap as high as
himself upon his head, and suitable clothes
upon his shoulders, and he stood respectfully
before them.   Then Jewād thus commanded
him : ' Khayālī Chawush, thou shalt go forth

and traverse the whole face of the earth, and
of every noble and high-born damsel, worthy
to be married to myself, whom thou dost see
among the pure virgins, ladies of beauty and
loveliness, of all the nations who dwell in the
Inhabited Quarter, thou shalt paint the likeness, each on a separate sheet of paper, and
write down her name and fame and age and
city and parish ; and bring these to me forthwith.' And the dwarf said, ' Command and
decree are of our lord,' and he kissed the
ground and departed. An hour had not
passed ere he returned with a box upon his
shoulders, which he placed beside Jewād.
The latter opened the box and called Emīn
and Ibrāhīm Chelebi to come and see ; and
they were engrossed with the spectacle.
First they saw the picture of a soul-ravishing
maiden which bewildered the understanding,
and there-under was written : ' This is the
portrait of Ferah-Nāz, the daughter of Lārī
Khān the present monarch of the kingdom
of Cathay, and she dwells in the imperial
palace of the City of Pekin : her age is

seventeen, and her height a builder's cubit
and four-and-fifty ells.' After looking at
this picture they lifted it up, and beneath it
was a portrait still more beautiful, on which
the name, abode, rank, age, and height were
detailed in like manner. They took from
under it another picture, which when Emīn's
eyes beheld, he became himself like a lifeless
picture, and fell down in a swoon. Jewād
and Ibrāhīm Chelebi on seeing this, sprinkled
rose-water upon his face and brought him to
himself. When Jewād read beneath the picture this description: 'This is the portrait of
Khayāl Khānim, daughter of 'Abbās Agha
of the chartered fief-holders, who dwells in
the City of Aleppo in the Rehāvī quarter,'
he knew the reason of Emīn's fainting, and
he was pleased. 'My Emīn,' said he, 'if it
be thus, good tidings to thee, thy desire is
accomplished;' and he gave him glad news
and comforted him. 'Brother,' continued
he, 'be it known unto thee that of every
form produced by sorcery or enchantment,
there must of necessity be some original

exactly similar ; but I feared lest what thou
hadst seen were the image of one dead:
thank God that that Khayāl Khānim whom
thou didst see and fall in love with is now
alive ; henceforth shall she be thy real wife.
An it be thy will, I shall cause her now to be
brought hither, but I would that I should
accomplish it without letting the clue become
public ; so, pray, for a few days have
patience.' Then he turned the reins of discourse to another quarter. They remained
there enjoying themselves till nearly ten
o'clock, when Jewād said, 'O brothers, it is
time for us to return to our homes ; do you
go first.' And the body of pages escorted
Ibrāhīm Chĕlebi and Emīn with honour as
far as the gate, then they went to the landing-
stage of Hayder Pasha, got into their boat,
and returned each to his house.

All that night till morning, sleep came not
to the eyes of Emīn or Ibrāhīm Chelebi, for
they remained imagining and marvelling,
and mazed and wondering. They went to
the shop, and while they were sitting silent

E ‹

and overpowered from the perfectness of
their bewilderment, musing upon the events
that had occurred, Jewād appeared before the
shop in his ordinary guise, gay and happy,
joyous and smiling; and he saluted them
and came in and sat down. Ibrāhīm Chelebi
prepared coffee, and departing not in any
wise from his usual wont, he made no slip
in appearing as though he had seen nought
of what had happened. Some hours later,
when the rest of the companions had dispersed, and only the three remained in the
shop, Jewād said to Ibrāhīm Chelebi, 'O
brother, Emīn is anxious now, let us get for
him his darling; but I pray that you follow
my plan in this matter.' Ibrāhīm answered,
'On head and eye;'* and Jewād thus instructed him : '*If it please God (exalted be
He !)*, do thou rent to-morrow a large mansion and get for thyself and Emīn some suits
of clothes such as are worn by grandees;
procure likewise two horses, some servants,

---

* *I.e.*, most willingly.

and all other needful things ; and give thyself out as a farmer of revenues ; go to the
requisite places, and doubling or tripling the
present sum, request the Collectorship of
Aleppo. Heed not how the money goes ; I
will send a slave to thy side who shall always
provide the needful amount ; when thou hast
got the Collectorship, we shall see each other
and talk further.' So saying, he arose and
went away.

The next morning Ibrāhīm Chelebi went
forth his house and proceeded to the Suley-
māniyya quarter, and asked from the imām
of the Cherry Mosque* the hire of a mansion
of twenty rooms. The imām went with him
till they came to a lofty house opposite the
Aqueduct. When they had looked over
the house, the imām said, ' Its rent is two
hundred and fifty piastres a-month ; but six
months' rent is required in advance, and until
it be received I cannot give up the key.'
Ibrāhīm Chelebi began to think, ' Truly we

* The Kirāzli Mesjidi, built by the Su-bashi Sunleymā.

ought not to have sought a house till we had
gotten the money,' and was thus pondering
when some one touched his arm. He turned
to see who it was, and beheld one of the
slaves with fur-trimmed caps whom he had
previously seen with Jewād. The slave said,
' My master, shall I give the money to the
imām ?' and he drew from his breast a purse
which might contain three thousand piastres
in shining Venetian sequins, and counted the
money into the imām's hand. He then took
the key and thrust it into his girdle, and said,
' O my master, your slave shall bring uphol-
sterers to furnish the house ; do you go to
the bazaar and buy raiment and other things
according to your taste, your slave, too, shall
come behind you.' Ibrāhīm Chelebi went to
the shop and informed Emīn of all that had
happened, and took him with him to the
bazaar, and when they purchased garments
the slave appeared and paid the money. In
short, after buying all manner of things they
went to the mansion, which they found
garnished with furniture of great price. In

three or four such days they had a magnificent establishment with slaves, horses, and
all accessories ; and Ibrāhīm Chelebi and
Monla Emīn, giving out that that they were
father and son, attired themselves in the
style of the highest nobles of the capital.
After finding out about it, Ibrāhīm Chelebi,
offering much in addition to the amount of
the former year, requested the Collectorship
of Aleppo.   He gave the money to the
officials in advance, and was arrayed in a
robe of honour and appointed Collector of
Aleppo.

Some days afterwards appeared Jewād,
crying, '*Hū! 'Azīzim ! ey-v'allāh !*'* with a
Bektāshī turban on his head, a neat robe
upon his shoulders, a white cloth cloak and
other dervish gear ; and he said, ' Welcome,
my master.' Ibrāhīm Chelebi and Emīn
Efendi rose to the saint with all honour and
respect. The attendants and others present,
imagining him to be the sheykh of His

* Pious ejaculations used by dervishes.   The Bektāshī
Order of dervishes is one of the most celebrated,

Excellency the Agha, stood reverently with
hands folded across the girdle. When they
were alone, Jewād said, ' O brothers, henceforward it is necessary that I be with you ;
when the time comes take a largish ship and
we shall go to the desired quarter. Do you
give me a room apart, but show me no
greater respect than is usually accorded
sheykhs, lest the people become curious.'
So he retired to a private room. When the
time for taking possession of the Collectorship drew nigh, they hired a special ship, in
which they embarked and set off in the
desired direction.

With favouring weather they reached
Aleppo in a short time, and, spreading the
carpet of ease and repose, busied themselves
with delight. As there was no registry of
capital, they laid the foundations of friendship and familiarity, and showed to every
person the greatest kindness. They became
acquainted with the grandees and notables,
and prepared banquets in the gardens, and so
won the heart of each individual that they

became the beloved of high and low. Market and bazaar, khan and house, coffee-house and tavern, were filled with lauds and praises of the virtues of the Collector.

As every one was pleased some way or other to meet Jewād, the original cause of their coming, 'Abbās Agha himself, one day came to visit them. What did they see? —there was no need of question or of divination, he was altogether the person they had seen before ; there was not a hair's difference in his circumstances, motions, speech, or appearance; there was but this much difference, that he did not know them or salute them, otherwise his actions were exactly those or the well-known 'Abbās Agha whom they had seen in the Sublime Capital. As much friendliness was manifested on both sides, 'Abbās Agha was again, after a lapse of two days, summoned before them. After having invited him a few times to their parties, where they treated him with kindness, he became an every-day visitor. Particularly, as he perceived that Jewād Baba, the Col-

lector's sheykh, was a possessor of understanding and an unequalled sage, he would
hardly ever be away from his virtuous society.
So one day Jewād opened the mouth of
wisdom, and began to disclose what was in
his heart, saying to 'Abbās Agha, ' Father,
Agha, it is well known to you that our Collector's son Emīn Efendi is a polite and
intelligent person ; certain of the grandees of
the Sublime Empire wished him for son-in-
law ; but as the ways of the Capital are dis-
pleasing to my poor taste, I would not
consent to his marrying. I have heard that
my lord has a virtuous daughter, and have
enquired into the matter, and made sure.
Now my wish is to make him son-in-law to
you, with the condition that even should
Ibrāhīm Agha be dismissed (which will not
be the case) Emīn Efendi continue to abide
in Aleppo ; that is, that he take not your
daughter to the Capital, but remain beside
you.'   Well, after some discussion, they
agreed upon the amount of the stipulated
dower ; and Khayāl Khānim daughter of

'Abbās Agha was married to Emīn Efendi.
Tents were pitched in front of the convent
of Sheykh Bekr ; and rope-dancers, jugglers,
acrobats, dancers, conjurors, minstrels, and
players afforded entertainment. At night
all sorts of fireworks were displayed ; and
thus for a whole week all the people, high
and low, enjoyed themselves with feasts and
music. On the completion of the wedding
ceremonies in this fashion, with prayers and
blessings they conducted Emīn Efendi to the
nuptial-chamber of his wishes. When, after
performing the wedding prayer, he raised the
veil from the face of the bride and saw his
wife who a year ago had died and for whom
he had longed and yearned so much, now his
senses fled away, leaving him bewildered, and
now he became excited, sighing and crying.
However, he praised and thanked God, and
remained in perfect delight till morning, sleep
entering not his eyes. For the purpose of
thanking, he went before his master, and first
kissed the hand of Jewād and received his
blessing, next he kissed that of Ibrāhīm Agha

who acted as his kind father ; and then went back to his beloved. For three weeks he remained in the bridal apartments without coming forth ; and afterwards he occupied himself attending the meetings held by his father and the sheykh.

About a month after his marriage, Jewād called Ibrāhīm Chelebi and Emīn Efendi before him, and, after a few introductory words, said, ' O brothers, you know how ' every union hath its parting ; ' the necessity of travel has become manifest to your slave. It is needful that, with your permission, I set forth to journey. I confide you to God. For as long as you wear the borrowed robe of life in this transient world, to my master 50,000 and to Emīn Efendi 50,000, together 100,000 piastres a-year, has been appointed as income. On the first day of Muharrem, which is the beginning of the year, that slave whom you know shall come, through power, to the place where you are, and give the money into your hands ; so you will not be troubled about the necessities of life. Forget me not in your prayers.' And he joined himself to a caravan about to go into the land of Persia, leaving Ibrāhīm Agha and Emīn Efendi in the corner of separation, and set forth with the desire of travelling through this perishing world.

So let the wonder-working Jewād remain viewing the power of God, wandering through towns and cities.

THE STORY OF FERAH-NAZ, THE DAUGHTER OF THE KING OF CHINA.

Thus doth the sweet-tongued reed relate and narrate another wondrous tale :—Lārī Khan, King of the realms of China, had a lovely daughter named Ferah-Nāz, the fame of whose beauty and grace and charms and elegance resounded through the world. Though the comeliness of her person thus threw cities into confusion, her nature and character were so sweet and pleasant that the neighbouring emperors and kings desired her in marriage, and sought for union with

her, expending the coin of their lives. But
Ferah-Nāz misliked the companionship of
men, and chose, like the Virgin Mary, the
corner of maidenhood. Her aged father was
displeased at this her conduct, and, summoning Libāba, his daughter's nurse, to a private
interview, he said, 'No one save thou can
discover what is the reason and cause of this
girl's unwillingness to marry. I wish thee to
find out what it is. If she desire not any of
the kings and vezirs, but has some one other
in view, there is no hindrance; howsoever
mean a person he may be, it were an easy
matter for our royal power to exalt him and
render him fit to be her mate ; only I wish
to behold a grandson. Thou must discover
what Ferah-Nāz has on her mind, and inform
us concerning it.' And he strongly urged
this upon Libāba. She accepted the King's
command, but said, ' My master, your handmaid shall undertake to unveil the mind and
thoughts of Ferah-Nāz ; but it is known to
Your Majesty that Her Highness the Princess
is not as other women : she is a lady endowed

with high qualities, upright, learned, versed
in the general and special sciences, acquainted with the ways of the world, and skilled in
polite disputation ; she will not easily give
up her secret ; I pray of your favour that you
hurry me not.'

When she obtained permission, she returned to her establishment, and, after countless reflections, when it was evening she went,
as of wont, to the room of Ferah-Nāz to pass
the night. She sat down, and, after many
pleasant words, conformably to the saying
'speech leads to speech,' she brought about
an opportunity and said to Ferah-Nāz with
tearful eyes and mournful face, 'My mistress,
I have a question to ask of you, an it vex not
your gentle mind.' '*I seek pardon of God*,
speak,' answered the Princess. So the nurse
thus began her task : ' My mistress, in ancient
times and past ages many and many lovers
and loved ones came into this world, the
histories of most of whom your handmaid
has studied ; some thousands of stories concerning them remain in the memory of your

well-wisher. Each one had a confidant, a
sympathising friend, a self-sacrificer—such
was the wont of those of yore. But my
opinion and belief is this, that not one of
those of old time had a slave, a tender handmaid, a proved concealer of secrets, like this
slave of yours; now, certain actions of my
mistress have made her handmaid heart-
sore.' Thus going straight to her aim, she
sought to fathom Ferah-Nāz, and continued:
' My mistress, many times the neighbouring
princes, especially the son of the King of
Ceylon, who is in beauty unique in the age,
have sought you in marriage; since your
answers to all have been absolute despair,
grief of heart has overtaken your handmaid.
So long as we wear the robe of humanity do
human impulses and carnal cravings encircle
all of us. And while it is apparent that there
must be some hidden reason for this choice
of singleness, why confide you not to your
handmaid the search for the remedy of your
secret grief, but treat her like a stranger?'

Ferah-Nāz smiled wonderingly and said

to her nurse with a countenance of displeasure, ' O lady, mother, you know this
your daughter to be a lady of understanding,
yet you imagine that she is as the daughters
of the people, swayed by the flesh and overcome of carnal desires.   But it is evident
from your words (seeing that you have never
before during so long a time spoken of this
matter, and to-night with an excuse so feeble
make thus bold an enquiry) that your auda-
city arises not merely from your own zeal,
but is to increase the knowledge of my kind
and gracious father.   Still, as you are so
urgent in your questioning, it is needful that
I disclose to you what is on my mind :—One
night, three years ago, I saw in a vision a
prince, peerless in beauty, hard by a garden;
never in my life had I beheld the like of him.
With the longing of humanity I was bewildered at his beauty, when of a sudden, while
I was gazing upon him, two deer, a buck and
a doe, came into the garden.   The buck
began to run about, but his foot got caught
in a snare, which when the doe saw, she came

and brake the snare, and set free her mate.
They had not gone two steps ere the doe
was likewise caught in a trap, and though
she showed her distress, the buck cared not
about his comrade's capture, but ran off
and left her. When I awoke from sleep I
thought much and interpreted my dream as
a celestial warning to me that if they were
to offer me a mate, even though fair as he
whom I had seen, I should not accept him ;
for husbands show no constancy towards
their wives. Behold, by reason of this celestial warning I cannot marry ; do you, my
mother, and you, my kind father, both give
up this fancy ; for your counsel and advice
can in no wise take effect.'

The nurse, after many excuses for her former speech, said, ' My mistress, if leave be
given to me your handmaid, I pray you
graciously to reflect upon my humble words.
I can prove that this vision you have related
is not divine ; for the glorious Creator of
men and jinn has made the coupling of
male and female the visible cause of the

existence of these countless, numberless creatures. It is evident that such a warning were contrary to the will of the Creator ; it is apparent upon the least reflection that this vision is a Satanic deception, which, fixing itself thus firmly in your noble and virtuous mind, has caused you, my mistress, to forget the pleasure of your parents and the pleasure of God. The apprehension and delusion which causes you to oppose your father's pleasure is clearly an instigation of the devil. Moreover, I can conclusively and surely prove that men are more constant in their troth than women ; a true example of my humble assertion is the story of Khoja 'Abdu-'llāh which I can relate to the Princess :—

THE STORY OF KHOJA 'ABDU-'LLAH.

" One day, while Hārūnu-'r-Reshīd, who was the most bounteous, illustrious, and upright of the 'Abbāsī Khalifs, and in every way the most munificent in generosity of his predecessors or successors, was conversing

F

with Ja'fer, his vezir, he vaunted himself
much on his beneficence and liberality, and,
forgetting himself, said, 'Is there in this age
anyone more bountiful than we or more
lavish in generosity to the world?' Ja'fer
boldly replied, 'My master, there is in Basra
a man of good family whom they call Khoja
'Abdu-'llāh; and if all the rulers of the earth
were to assemble together and exert every
effort thereto, they could not give away as
much wealth as he bestows on the deserving
in a single day.' Hārūn's heart was con-
tracted at these words, and saying, 'If that
be so, it has become imperative to go to
Basra and see this man,' he disguised himself
as a qalender,* and set out with two trusty
servants; and arrived at Basra.

    "On asking of one of the people, according
to the wont of strangers, which of the cara-
vanseries, that is khans, was suitable to their
circumstances, the man replied, 'Holy men,
Khoja 'Abdu-'llāh has special guest-houses

---

* A wandering dervish.

in this place, faqīrs like yourselves ought
not to go elsewhere ; come, my fathers, I
will conduct you.' And he led them to a
great gate. When the attendants of the
guest-house, who were set apart for this duty
saw the dervishes, ten of them came forth
the gate and met them with the greeting,
'Welcome, and fair welcome;' and they took
them to a room in an upper storey. From
the furniture of the room, Hārūn imagined it
to be one of the Khoja's private apartments.
Straightway attendants brought in basin and
ewer, and washed the dust of the road from
their faces. After coffee and pipes,* came
three trays of delicious and delicate foods,
which were placed on the stools and partaken of; and as night was come, clean, fresh
beds were spread, and they rested in sweet
sleep till morning. Then one of the attendants came and said, 'My lord, the guest-

---

* This is, of course, an anachronism ; coffee and tobacco
were not in use till long after the close of the 'Abbāsī
Khalifate ; but this story, like all the others (except the
incident of the Chinese priests), illustrates old Turkish life.

house has a private bath, pleasant and
cleanly ; if you have a mind thereto, pray,
come.' Hārūn, to whom observation was as
a second nature, arose and went to the bath
with the attendant. He saw it to be a bath
the like of which did not then exist in
Baghdād, the Abode of the Khalifate. With
all respect the attendants of the bath led the
sheykh to a bench, stript him of his dervish
robe and wrapped him in heavy towels and
brought him into the warm-bath apartment,
where two lovely servants rubbed and washed
him with bag and soap, and then perfumed
him with aloes-wood and ambergris, and led
him into the dressing-room. There they
dried him gently, put on his clothes, and,
having conducted him back to his room, prepared breakfast, which he partook of and
then rested.

"Three days passed thus, and on the
fourth he said to one of the attendants, 'This
courtesy and kindness is good, but cannot
we see our host Khoja 'Abdu-'llāh ?' The
servant answered on this wise, 'The Khoja

has thus directed us:—"Trouble not any of
the guests by saying, 'Go to the Khoja,' unless
he desire to come to us:" therefore it de-
pends upon your wish—if it be your desire,
come, I shall take you.' Hārūn left his companions in the guest-house and went alone;
they entered through a great gate into a vast
and spacious court, in which stood ready harnessed about a hundred Arab horses tied in
a row and decorated with princely saddles
and caparisons. When they perceived the
guest, many handsomely-dressed attendants,
of the attendants of the palace, came forward
to greet him, and, taking hold of his skirt
and arms, reverently led him up. He saw a
lofty saloon containing about forty doors,
over each of which was hung a curtain, like
the canopy of a throne, all of one colour, and
he judged each curtain to be worth a hundred purses. They raised one of the curtains
and said, 'Go forward.' When he entered
the room, its adornment with decorations such
as cannot be described plunged Hārūn into
amazement. On seeing his guest, the Khoja

advanced to the threshold of the room, saying, 'My master, father, sultan, you have
honoured us ; all hail !' And he seated
Hārūn in the place of honour, and sat down
near him, and began to entreat him with
courtesy and kindness.

" After coffee and sherbets had been drunk
and other ceremonies of that time observed,
the Khoja said, ' Come, my lord, let us eat,'
and he led him into another room more magnificent than the first, and they sat down at
a spread table and partook of food. Let us
not expatiate on the qualities of the meats
or the description of the vases and vessels.
When finished they went into another room
and gave themselves up to ease ; Khoja
'Abdu-'llāh, begging to be excused, asked,
' My saint, whence have you brought honour?
Of what land are you a son ? ' ' My master,
replied Hārūn, ' our name is Muhammed,
and our land Baghdād the Abode of the
Khalifate.' The Khoja manifested great
delight, and said, 'My saint, you are a fellow-
townsman ; your slave too is originally of

Baghdād,' and they continued to converse
earnestly and profoundly. The Khoja intro-•
duced the subject of objects of vertu, and'said,
' My lord, it is true that there are no curiosities the like of which may not be found in
the Abode of the Khalifate ; but this poor
slave of yours has a jewelled image of a
lemon-tree which is in his belief a rarity.'
' Bring it,' cried he, ' and let the father, my
fellow-townsman, see it.'   A Cathayan slave-
boy, a loveling of world-disturbing beauty,
whose like for comeliness Hārūn had never
seen in all his life, clad in costly garments,
brought in a curiosity of immense value, a
flower-pot formed of a single ruby in which
was a large tree, the branches whereof were
made of gold, the blossoms of diamonds, the
leaves of emeralds, the lemons of topazes,
and the oranges of rubies.   The boy kissed
the skirt of the sheykh's robe and placed the
tree beside him for examination.   While
Hārūn was wondering whether to look at the
boy or inspect the tree, the Khoja said, 'Take
it away.'   ' By God, my master,' said the

sheykh, 'the truth is this, that that is a curiosity such as exists not in the Khalifs
treasury. 'My lord,' replied the other, 'while
you are with your slave there is always by
him an object of virtue.' 'Bring that parrot-
cage!' Immediately there appeared a slave-
girl, more beautiful than the boy, adorned
with ornaments and decorations, bearing a
cage, which she placed beside the sheykh,
whose hand she kissed. It was a cage em-
bellished with peerless jewels, and in it was
a parrot, formed from one emerald, which
every quarter of an hour spake in a strange
tongue. It also they left but a very brief
while, and then bore away. Six such wonderful curiosities were seen, three of which
were brought by boys and three by damsels.
Hārūn grew angry and said in himself, 'It
beseems not the rank of this fellow that he
unseasonably shows off curiosities for glory
among men ;' and he asked permission to
depart. 'By God, my brother!' said the
Khoja, 'I pray that you will honour me

again;' and he accompanied him to the door of the room.

"When Hārūn descended to the horse-block they brought forward one of the choice steeds, and mounted him thereon, and two servants, marching at his stirrups, conducted him to the guest - house. On entering the room, what did he behold?—the three damsels and the three boys, along with the curiosities he had seen, were standing in the apartment. One of the boys had a note in his hand which he presented to Hārūn, and in it was written : ' The following trifling objects are presented to Sheykh Muhammed, of Baghdād, by Khoja 'Abdu-'llāh on the second day of such and such a month :—slave-girls, three ; beardless slave-youths, three ; Cossack slaves attired as servants, two ; curiosities, six ; caparisoned horse, one ; sequins for one month's expenses, five thousand.' When Hārūn read this note his senses were bewildered, and he said in himself, ' That he should give such objects to a miserable Bektāshī is a thing which cannot come within the scale of understanding ; there must be some hidden mystery here, but until I disclose myself to the Khoja it is manifestly impossible to learn his secret.   But to disclose myself in this state were derogatory to the dignity of the Khalifate ; it were more becoming to hasten forthwith to Baghdād, and, summoning Khoja 'Abdu-'llāh to the Abode of the Khalifate, ask of him his secret and so solve the puzzle.'

"The next day he set out ; and when he reached Baghdād he informed Ja'fer of what had happened.   So an order was written to bring thither Khoja 'Abdu-'llāh with all becoming respect and honour, and one of the chamberláins was despatched.   In twenty days, the chamberlain returned and reported that, three days before his reaching Basra, Khoja 'Abdu-'llāh had passed away to the Abode of Permanency, and that therefore meeting with him was deferred till the Resurrection - Day.   The Khalif mourned passing sore at this news, and bewailed the **death** of **Khoja** ·Abdu-'llāh.

"A year and three months after this, a son named Me'mūn* was born to Hārūn, and one day while the month of festivities was in progress, when dancers were performing at the Imperial palace and a great throng of people was assembled to see them, one of the slaves whom Khoja 'Abdu-'llāh had pre-sented to the Khalif perceived 'Abdu-'llāh in the dress of a beggar, standing among the spectators. He went to his side and said, ' My master, is it thou?' And, waiting not while 'Abdu-'llāh said this thing and that thing, he ran off and told the Khalif. Hārūn despatched an officer along with the slave, telling the former to bring the person whom the latter pointed out. Whenever the Khalif saw him he recognised him beyond all doubt, and ordered him to sit down ; and he dis-played all manner of kindness towards him, with honour and respect. After his fears had been dispelled, he sent him to the bath and clad him in one of his own suits of clothes.

* He was afterwards Khalif.

Hārūn dined with him and removed all cares
of ceremony and pomp, and retired into a
private room with Ja'fer and 'Abdu-'llāh, and,
spreading the carpet of familiarity, said,
'O Khoja 'Abdu-'llāh, knowest thou me?'
'My lord,' replied the Khoja, 'how should
not I know you? no one can doubt that you
are our lord who now sits upon the Throne
of the Khalifate, that your slave should not
know you.' 'Nay,' said Hārūn, 'but have
you never seen me before, in another place,
and in other guise?' 'No, my lord,' was the
reply, and the Khoja pondered. Then the
Khalif explained to him how he had gone,
expressly to see him, in the dress of a
qalender: how he had lodged in his guest-
house, how he had been treated by him with
exceeding kindness, and how he had, in con-
sequence, sent an officer to summon him who
had brought back word of his death. Next
he asked the cause of all that had happened,
and said, 'What is the reason of your now
coming hither in beggar's guise, of your
having fallen into this poverty and penury,

while you used to be possessor of so great
wealth?' 'My lord,' replied he, 'the adventures of your slave are marvellous, and his
experiences wonderful ; if it weary you not,
he shall relate what has befallen him from
the commencement of his fortunes till this
hour.' Permission being accorded, he thus
began his story.

"'There was in the Abode of the Khalifate,
during the reign of your departed father, a
famous merchant, by name Nasr. I am his
son. On the death of my father, I was only
sixteen years old ; a youth, beautiful and
comely, inclined to pleasure and mirth, heed-
less of the heat and cold of fortune. Thinking not of the extent of the vast wealth
which my father had earned by the labour
of his right hand and the sweat of his brow,
I wasted and squandered and lavished and
lost it, and sank so low that I considered
with myself how it were better to die in a
foreign land than to live in degradation
among my associates and equals. So, saying to myself, ' I have no resource but

travel,' I became servant to one of a caravan about to start, and went into Egypt.

"'The day we entered Cairo, I left my companions, and set out alone to see the bazaars of the city. While I was wandering aimlessly along, my eyes fell upon a houri-like damsel about to shut a window in a lofty mansion. A single glance at her so took me out of myself that my senses and reason and understanding passed away, and I fell upon the ground. I lay on the street for about an hour unconscious, like a lifeless figure. When my senses were in a measure returned, I reasoned strenuously with myself, and, rushing away, went back to the khan where we had alighted with the caravan. Free from all thoughts of food or drink, I remained that night in a corner, reasoning with myself till dawn. Now tears overcame me, and I would weep, and now reason got the upper hand, and I would say, 'O luckless one! it sufficeth not that, fallen into the dust of degradation and sunken from affluence to indigence, covered with

shame and disgrace among thy comrades,
thou hast had to choose exile and banish-
ment, struggling on. What hath befallen
thee that thou must become enamoured of
a form concerning which thou knowest
nothing—above all, as it is manifest from
its embellishments and walls that the mansion in which thou sawest the phantom is
the establishment of one of the greatest of
the grandees of this country? Setting that
aside, and supposing she were the daughter
of one of the lowest and meanest of the
people, thou couldst not marry her. Who
would have aught to do with thee in such a
guise—who would look upon thee in such
rags? This is a vain thing, the result of thy
calamities. The Tempter hath taken the
form of a woman to plunge thee into the
abyss of ruin, he is so eager for thy life.'

" 'Howsoever much I strove to shake off
and forget my longing, showing its futility
to my unhappy self, it was vain ; and when
the dawn appeared I arose, and again went
straight to opposite the window, and sat

down, and, after the manner of beggars, bowing my head, besought alms of the passers-by. But of what use? It was impossible for me to withdraw my eyes for a single moment from the window. Food and drink passed altogether away from my mind. In the evening I went to the khan, and in the morning to the corner opposite the window; and seven days passed thus distractedly, and I neither ate nor drank. At length my frame grew so weak that I was unable to return to the khan, when, lo! an old woman came forth with a bowl of soup and a loaf of fine bread in her hand, which she placed before me, and said, 'They have sent thee this bread and soup from the palace which is opposite; take and eat.' From the greatness of my joy and delight, I ate. She took the bowl, and asked, 'Whence art thou?' I told her that I was of a strange country, and informed her of the khan where I passed the night. And she put ten sequins into my hand, and said, 'Take these, and go to the khan where thou lodgest, and come hither no more.'

"'Having no resource, I returned to the khan weeping, and sat down, sad and sorrowful, in my accustomed corner. I mourned, sighing, 'Would to God that I had died of my hunger opposite to my beloved!' And thus the night passed. When it was morning, I saw the old woman coming again with soup and fine bread in her hand, and she placed them beside me, and saluted me, and said, 'O hapless one, how art thou?' My hands and feet trembled through joy, and I began to weep. She asked, 'Who art thou, and from what land art thou come, and what business hast thou here?' So I narrated to her briefly my fortunes and adventures. When she said, 'What is the cause of thy being thus ill?' I, fearing to reveal, remained silent. 'Be not afraid,' said she, 'I am none of the indiscreet; relate to me thy woes.' So, with a thousand writhings, I loosed the collar of speech, and hinted how I had encountered a

G

' phantom from behind the veil. Driving horses over me, she compelled me to speak plainly and confess all ; and then she said, ' O unhappy one, that mansion which thou sawest is the palace of Mansūr-Bi-'llāh, the present Sultan of Egypt, and that damsel is one of his favourite slave-girls ; to turn thy thoughts to thus impossible a fancy is unlawful for a man like thee, and an abyss of ruin. It were best to drive these frightful thoughts altogether from thy mind, and to occupy thyself with some work that will earn thy daily bread.' Smiling sadly, I replied, ' O my mistress, mother, lady—all these words are vain. What fear? What ruin? What daily bread? My work is finished. I knew from the beginning that this fancy was vain. But this matter is from Destiny. For me there is no remedy save to die thinking on the loved one, and, in the Hereafter, to be raised with Mejnūn and Ferhād and Wāmiq and 'Azrā*—one of the victims of Love. The

* The names of famous lovers in the Eastern romances.

time for advice is past. But I beg of you, my mother, that, if you bring me this bread and soup out of charity, you will, to favour me, bring it no more; for the cursed flesh cannot refrain from eating, and if I eat but once in three or four days the event will be delayed, and you will be guilty; for to die were to me great joy—do not, with your soup and bread, deprive me of that joy.'

"'When I had, with fervour like to that, told the old woman what lay on my heart, she was constrained to tears, and full bitterly did she weep for my case; and she took the bowl and went away. Although hopeless of ever possessing the beauty of the beloved, yet the learning who was my hitherto unknown mistress was that night a fresh wound in my heart, and yet a plaything.

"'When it was morning, the old woman again appeared, at the same hour as before, with soup and a package in her arms. I cried, 'Why have you brought this, and not listened to my request?' and would have repulsed her, but she said, 'Take the soup

this time, and be not rebellious, for that
beauty, the love of whom has enslaved thee,
sends thee greeting.'   When she uttered
these words, trembling seized my whole
frame from head to foot ; and the bird, the
soul, was well-nigh released from its cage,
the body.   Who could have looked at the
soup ?   I gazed at the source of the water of
life, the lips of the old woman, to see if there
might be there another blessing.   Power of
motion departed from me, but the old woman
roused me from my bewilderment, and said,
'I have somewhat that has been confided to
me to say to thee, but do thou first collect
thy senses that thou mayst understand the
words I am about to speak.'   At these glad
tidings I came to myself; and when I appeared tranquil the old woman thus addressed
me: 'Son, there is no doubt that thy fortunes are of the hidden providence of God.
She whom thou hast seen, and whom I have
told thee to be of the favourite slave-girls
of the Sultan of Egypt, is a pure virgin, a
maiden modest as Mary, by name Durr-

Dāna. Two years ago, the Sultan of Egypt
purchased her, and enrolled her among his
wives ; but when she saw how much he inclined to other damsels, she repulsed his
advances and opposed him, saying, 'Thou
mayst slay me, but I will not submit to
thee.' She has persisted in this attitude for
two years, but by reason of her beauty and
grace the Sultan of Egypt cannot bring himself to expel her ; and they are still in this
contention. One day, when great weariness
and vexation had come upon her, after the
noon worship, she recited many supereroga-
tory prayers, and, weeping, raised her hands
to the Court of the Creator of all beings, and
said, 'Make me the mate of a poor man, but
constant, though the meanest of all the
people, rather than the wife of thus faithless
a Sultan, who knows not true worth.' And
she humbled herself and wept, and thereupon
she opened the window and beheld thee ;
and thou sawest her. And there came this
thought into her sad heart—'Lo ! meaner
and poorer than yon man there cannot be,

yet am I content with him, so that he be but
of those that are constant.' She went the
next day to the window for a diversion, and
beheld thee gazing abstractedly thereat, and,
looking upon thee with attention, she perceived that no other action proceeded from
thee, and that thy eyes were ever fixed upon
the window. Then she knew that the prayer
she had made in sincerity had met with the
Divine acceptance, and that thou hadst become enamoured of her at a single glance.
After this, she watched thee for some days,
and she wept, and love for thee took root in
her breast. Fearing lest if thou were observed gazing at the harem windows they
would persecute thee, she sent me with the
soup and supplies, and ordered that thou
shouldst not return. When I told her all
thy case, and how that thy death was at
hand if she delayed, putting aside all other
fears, she sent me to inform thee of the position. She has sent thee a suit of clothes and
a hundred sequins, and begs that thou wilt
repair to the bath, and cleanse thee, and

put on these clothes, and enjoy thyself for
four or five days in ease, and collect thy
senses, and be hopeful of union with thy
beloved.   And when thou art all recovered
and rested we shall think upon some plan.'

"'The joy that came upon me at this intelligence will be understood of him who has
loved a darling and fallen in the wilderness
of woe.   I straightway took the package,
kissed it, and raised it to my forehead.   And
I arose and, according to the command of
the beloved, went to the bath and cleansed
me of filth and mire, and put on the
clothes that had been presented to me, and
returned to the khan.   I passed that night
in perfect repose, and then began to think of
eating and drinking ; and waited from moment to moment, wondering what news
would come from the direction of the loved
one.   A week passed thus, when the old
woman again appeared and gave me new
life with salutations and greetings from the
beloved.   She said, ' Durr-Dāna desires to
converse with you.   See, I have brought you

a suit of female clothes and a cloak ; there is
an empty ruined mosque in such and such a
place,—come there,—I shall wait at the door
while you change your dress, for I must
conduct you to Durr-Dāna ; but be very
careful, for if it become known, our fate is
sealed.' I took the bundle of clothes, and we
went to the ruined mosque ; where I did off
my man's dress and arrayed myself as a
woman. As I was a beardless youth my
appearance in no wise differed from that of
a female when I had put on the cloak and
shawl ; and I walked by the side of the old
woman as though I were her daughter.

"'We entered the palace at the time of the
evening call to worship, and we passed into
a private room to the presence of Durr-Dāna.
When my eyes fell upon the face of my
beloved, my breath was stopped and my
senses fled away, and I fell to the ground.
The old woman sprinkled rose-water on my
face and brought me to myself again, and
seated me at the side of the room. When
my confusion was dispelled, Durr-Dāna

opened her gracious mouth and said, "'Abdu-
'llāh, behold, thy woes are ended.   But in
what way wilt thou be able to deliver me
hence ?   It is manifest that if I gave thee
money and thou were to go about to purchase
me, it would be impossible ; nothing remains
but to seek some means of flight.   If we
betake ourselves to some other country thou
wilt there marry me.   At present thou art
not calm enough to devise plans ; but reflect
well when alone.   I too shall consider ; we
can communicate by means of the old
woman, and then take flight.'

" ' Whilst we were talking, suddenly a noise
was heard in the vestibule ; and I saw the
Sultan of Egypt and twenty executioners,
with drawn swords, enter the room.   The
enemies of Durr-Dāna had been watching
and had given the clue.   The Sultan rushed
upon Durr- Dāna, crying, 'O ungrateful
wretch, is this the cause of thy aversion
towards me ?'   And as he raised his sword
the executioners caught his hand and said,
' Master, that work is ours, do not you stain

with blood your hand of glory!' He shouted,
'Take these wretches and bind their hands
and feet and cast them into the River Nile!'
So the executioners seized Durr-Dāna and
myself and made fast our hands and feet,
and, two of them taking us upon their shoulders, carried us to the brink of the Nile.
Having for so long looked for death, I had
no fear thereof; but I grieved for Durr-Dāna,
and begged the executioner who was carrying
me to cast me first into the river that I might
not see Durr-Dāna being drowned. He
granted my request, and, raising me up, hurled
me into the stream. I first sank to the
bottom, but rose again to the surface, and,
as it was the season of the overflow of the
Nile, I was borne along a great distance in
the twinkling of an eye. I was filled up to
throat with water and my eyes were dimmed,
when my foot got entangled at the ankle
with the root of a reed. Now some Arabs
who were fishing on the bank of the river
saw me struggling, and, thinking it to be a
fish, they came up to me. Seeing that the

vital spark was still within me, they drew me
out with the harpoon they had in their hands,
and stretched me upon the sand, and, pressing
my belly, got out the water I had swallowed ;
and they took off my wet clothes and clad
me in a dry shirt of their own. After a time,
my senses returned, and I grieved for that
I had been saved after Durr-Dāna had
perished, and I sorrowed for my life. But
what was the use? I thanked the fishermen,
and these put into my hand by way of
charity a sequin—one of those that had been
in my pocket, and said, ' Now stay not, but
be off.'

"' I fared on for about an hour, but through
sad sorrow and grief at parting from my
beloved, and the shock of drowning, my
strength was exhausted, and I sat down and
thought in myself, ' The only way possible
to join my loved one is to die and be united
with her in the Hereafter. Henceforward it
is unbecoming for me to live ; but to throw
myself into the River Nile and be drowned
were unlawful. All undesirous of the world,

my only resource is to retire into some corner
and await death from the anguish of separation.'   I cast away the sequin that was in
my hand, and went straight from the bank
of the Nile.   When it was near morning, I
happened to pass through a village, where I
met the imām going to mosque.   He, perceiving me to be a stranger, took me to the
mosque, and we together performed the
morning worship.   When it was finished, he
left me in the mosque, and went and brought
a platter of qusqus,* which I ate for his
sake.   Then he asked if I were going
to Rosetta, and when I replied that I was, he
said, 'We have a barge going there this day:
I shall put thee therein.'   So he called the
master and made me over to him.   When we
reached Rosetta, I got on board a ship going
to the Syrian Tripoli, where, on our arrival,
I joined a caravan, and wandered aimlessly
through cities and towns till I came to Basra.

"'Five months had now passed since I left

* Name of a dish.

Egypt, and I was beginning to recover and
regain my senses in a measure. I went to a
coffee-house, the keeper of which, when he
saw me, knew me to be a stranger, and entreated me kindly. After I had been for two
days a guest in the coffee-house, the keeper
said to me, 'Son, thou art a stranger here ;
if thou wilt be my apprentice, I will give
thee a monthly salary of so many piastres.'
'Most willingly,' replied I, 'but I want not
the salary ; it is enough if thou give me of
the food thou dost thyself eat.' And I
kissed his hand, and entered with assiduity
into service at the coffee-house.

"'Thousands of people came to the coffee-
house ; but there was one handsome, sweet-
spoken, elegantly-dressed man, called 'Alī
Efendi, who came regularly every day, and
spent each day five or ten piastres. As he
was a regular customer at the coffee-house, I
showed greater honour and attention to him
than to any of the others ; and he grew very
fond of me, and always treated me with kindness. One day, when we were alone in the

shop, he called me to his side, and gently
said, "'Abdu-'llāh, I doubt not that thou art
a high-born youth, but from what country
art thou and of whom art thou the son?' I
tried to evade, but it was no use, he persisted;
so, when I saw I could not help it, I related
to him in detail all that had befallen me. He
was silent, and remained for a long time
wondering and reflecting. A day or two
afterwards, again finding me alone, he said,
'Son, thou must be miserable in this coffee-
house; come and reside with me, and I will
make thee my son, and, *if it please God
(exalted be He!)*, thou shalt be happy.'
These words of the Efendi touched my
heart, and I kissed his hand; and he took
me thence to his house. He had ten or so
slaves besides myself. In very truth, that
man treated me in a fatherly manner, and
paid much attention to my education; he
made me go about in all sorts of magnificent
clothes, more sumptuous than his own, and
always seated me beside himself, and took
great care in teaching me to read and write.

"'Two years passed thus, when my master
'Alī Efendi fell ill, and day by day his feebleness increased upon him. When he had
reached the verge of dissolution and given
up hope of recovery, he called me to his
side, and having dismissed the other attendants, brought his face close to mine, and
said, 'My son, 'Abdu-'llah, I have a testa-
mentary bequest, a secret which I must make
known to thee ; but thou must swear and
convince me that thou wilt never disclose it
to anyone so long as thou livest.' When I
had sworn by God, the High, the Most High,
to conceal it, he continued, 'Son, I am possessor of a hidden treasure which has
descended from my ancestors ; since I have
no children it has been decreed to thee ; and
it is but for this trust that I have brought
thee up. When I am dead and buried, thou
wilt find it ; it is in such and such a place ;
open it and take out the amount of gold thou
mayst need, but take great care to avoid
waste and extravagance ; and beware of
going to its further extremity, for it is very

terrible : all of this did my father tell me.'
And he pulled out the key of the treasure
and gave it into my hand ; and a few hours
later he died and was buried with all fitting
pomp.

"'I freed all the male and female slaves who
were in the house, and presented them with
the carpets and vases that were therein, and
dismissed them.   As no one remained in the
house but myself, that night I took a candle
in my hand and entered the treasury.   I saw
it to be an underground place, like an arsenal,
a hundred and fifty cubits in length and
twenty cubits in breadth, and on either side
thereof were coins of gold and silver piled up
like wheat and barley.   I offered thanks to
God and said in myself, 'There is nothing
frightful here, although my master warned
me, let me go forward and see; it ill becomes
one to be afraid of things like these.'   So I
was constrained to penetrate to its depths,
and went on without fear. Squeezing myself
through a narrow door, I entered a portico in
which were some strange forms, which, in

truth, seemed very terrible; still, mustering
courage, I went through among the forms
and passed through a door at the other end
into a hall, forty cubits long and forty cubits
broad, all round which at intervals of one
cubit were shelves covered with curiosities,
wonders of the world, 'such as eye hath not
seen nor ear heard.'   Passing thence through
a door, I entered another hall as large as the
first, in the midst of which was a golden
tank, ten cubits by ten, filled to overflowing
with diamonds and rubies and emeralds and
other jewels, the very smallest of which
would be the envy of monarchs. There were
fifty doors round the hall, and in the centre
of it upon a throne on a dais were the statues
of a man and woman who supported a tablet
between them—the right hand of the one
being placed upon it, and the left hand of the
other.   I approached the statues and looked
at the tablet, and there was inscribed thereon
in a beautiful pendant hand:* ' Be it known

* The *Ta'liq*, or pendant, is a beautiful variety of hand-
writing, much used in fine manuscripts.

H

unto thee, O thou who hast come hither to visit us, that I am Melīqā, who for a thousand years was sovereign of the Nation of the Jinn, and that this is my wife Lāqiyūr. For nine hundred years I lived with this my wife on such happy and joyous wise that, unable to bear the sundering of death, I gathered all ٫my possessions into this place, and, having ordered that we should both be buried beneath this dais, poisoned myself. Each of the doors which thou beholdest is that of a treasure-hoard; and the understanding is unable to conceive the amount and extent of the riches here. But sages have reckoned thus: seeing that not more than a single man can pass through the second door at once, if the portals of this cavern were thrown open and permission accorded to all men to sack and plunder, it would require one hundred and twenty years to empty it.'

"'After reading the tablet, I went forth the cavern. My first thought was to erect mosques and soup-kitchens and guest-houses and other pious and charitable buildings to

the soul of Durr-Dāna.   In short, my opul-
ence and splendour and alms and bounties
and liberality grew so famous that they were
heard of and seen by Your Glorious Majesty.
There is no need for detail : a year passed
thus, when the circumstance of our magnificence was reported to 'Azadu-'d-Devlet, the
present King of Basra, and they denounced
me, saying, ' This man must indeed have
found a hidden treasure, it were well were—
you to call him before you and compel him
to discover it.'   So he sent a chamberlain
who brought me into his presence, when he
said to me, with all bitterness, 'Look, 'Abdu-
'llāh, denial is impossible for thee, thou hast
assuredly found a hidden treasure ; declare
where it is, else is there no escape for thee,
for I will slay thee cruelly.'   ' My master,'
replied I, ' I have indeed found a hidden
treasure ; but though you were to cut me into pieces, small even as my ear, it is impossible and inconceivable that I should disclose it.   Still, I shall make a compact with
you to send, so long as I live, a thousand

sequins a day to the royal treasury; if you
consent not, and insist on being shown the
cavern, your slave is prepared for death and
all manner of torture.   There is no need of
further speech.'   The King pondered, and I
made sure of death; but he agreed, and gave
into my hand a note in his own writing de-
claring that I should not be troubled or
molested either by himself or any other.
Ten years passed, without any negligence
in my performance of the contract.

"'Although I was in affluence, Durr-Dāna
was never absent a single moment from my
mind ; not only did I not marry, but though
I had numberless fair slave-girls, the thought
never occurred to me that there were women
and allurements to love in my establishment.
One night, between the two hours of worship,
while I was sitting still, a woman, in an old
veil and ragged dress, came into my house,
and kissed my hand.   I said to her, 'Daughter, what seekest thou ? '   She replied, ' My
master, pray come from the room, for I have
somewhat to say to you.'   When we had

passed into a private apartment, she threw
off her veil and cloak, and came and sat beside me. What did I see?—she was a lovely
beauty, such as the painter, the imagination,
were powerless to portray; in a moment
she overcame me, and drove the image of
Durr-Dāna from my mind. 'My master,'
said she, 'I, your handmaid, am your neigh-
bour here; seeing you, my master, from time
to time, I am become your devoted lover.
Although you have a thousand damsels like
to me, yet take compassion on me, and
favour me with permission to come every
four or five nights that I may behold the
beauty of my master.' I was amazed, but
took her by the hand and led her to a delightful room in the harem, and ordered
fruits and wine to be brought; and we began
to amuse ourselves. In the hilarity caused
by the wine, I threw my arm round her neck
to cull a kiss, when the damsel looked very
sad, and her eyes filled with tears. On beholding this the joyousness departed from
me, and I said to her, 'Speak truly, what is

the cause of this thy grief?' Then she fell to
weeping aloud, and, clasping my feet, kissed
them, and said, 'My master, it is vain, thou
art a man kind and honourable, I may not
conceal my secret from thee—if thou pity my
sad case, mercy is thine; if thou pity not,
command is thine; but if thou pity not,
woeful is my lot. I am Nā'ila, the daughter
of that shameless wretch, that infamous man,
called Elqam, who is Vezir to the present
King of Basra. I am now betrothed to a
noble youth named Emīr Hayder, and we
were to have been united, when that wretch,
my so-called father, envious of your wealth
and knowing that by reason of the letter the
King had given you promising that none
should molest you, it was impossible to
acquire knowledge concerning your cavern
by oppressing you, conceived the following
stratagem. He summoned me to his private
room and said, 'Thy beauty is unique in the
world; go to Khoja 'Abdu-'llāh in such and
such a dress and act in such and such a
manner, and even yield thyself to him, do

whatever is needful, only see where is his
hidden treasure, and come and tell me ; and
if thou succeed not in this undertaking, most
surely will I slay thee.' And he sware to do
so, and brought me himself as far as thy
door. Therefore do I weep; life is dear, yet
the preservation of the veil of honour is more
precious than the believer's blood. Mercy,
my master, I am in thy power, whatsoever
thou mayst deem fit, grace is thine!'

"'When she said this my heart bled, and I
replied, 'My daughter, henceforward art thou
my child; the protection of thy honour is my
bounden duty, and thy defence is incumbent
on my zeal. Fear not, be at ease. Willingly
shall I show thee that hidden treasure ; but
first I must blindfold thine eyes, and I shall
take a sword in my hand and hold it above
thy head, and lead thee to the hoard, and
show it all to thee ; but if, before I unbind
thine eyes, thou raise thy hand to free them,
I will slay thee without mercy, without pity.'
She agreed, and in that way I took her into
the cavern and showed it to her, and I said,

'Permission is thine, take whatsoever thou pleasest of these jewels.' And she filled her bosom and her pocket. There was round the neck of the statue of the King's wife a string of a hundred pearls, each large as a partridge's egg and each worth a treasure-hoard in itself; this I took from the neck of the statue and hung round that of the maiden. Again blindfolding her eyes as before, we returned to the house. I made her wrap herself in her cloak, and sent her with some trusty men to her father's abode.

" 'The infamous Vezir, having failed to discover the treasure by this stratagem, sold one of his slaves in the market. Our officer who purchased slaves bought him and brought him to our establishment. After a time he was placed among those slaves who prepared the food ; he watched his opportunity, and put some intoxicating drug upon a dish, of which I was very fond. When I rose after eating, a weakness came over my heart, and I fainted, exclaiming, ' I am dead.' They washed and shrouded me, and buried me in the mausoleum I had built. When it was evening that accursed one sent some disguised men, who conveyed me to another place. After they had tightly bound my hands and feet, they made me inhale some spirit, and brought back my senses. On waking I found myself in woeful case, the Vezir was standing opposite me with a whip in his hand, he addressed me thus, 'O wretch, I will teach thee to find a hidden treasure and then keep it all to thyself; come, where is the hoard?' I thought in myself how there was no escape from the fellow's hands, and severed the thread of hope, and returned no answer; but made sure of death, and repeated the words of the Profession of Faith. The pitiless wretch, enraged at my making no reply, beat me until he was exhausted, and said, 'There, think well, I shall not get tired, twice every day and every night will I beat thee thus, thou knowest if thou canst endure it; when thou tellest of the treasure thou shalt be freed;' and he left.

" 'Two hours afterwards, while I was groan-
ing under the pain of the wounds, I heard
some one open the door.   I imagined that
that wretch had returned, when there entered
the Vezir's daughter Nā'ila, and with her a
beardless youth, her husband, Emīr Hayder.
They both came up and unloosed my hands
and feet, and, weeping for my sad plight,
told me how the Vezir had got possession of
me by means of his slave who dressed my
food, how I had been buried, and how he had
spread among the folk the report of my
death, and then removed me from the tomb
and brought me hither.   But they had
a horse ready waiting, upon which they
mounted me, and, saying, ' Go, God be thy
helper!' sent me off.   Thanking and praising God, I galloped on, and in the morning
I dismounted at a certain place, and took a
short rest, and then set forth again.   I got
my wounds dressed at the villages on the
road ; and at length I arrived at the Abode
of the Khalifate.   To-day I came to the
palace to witness the pageant of Our Puissant

Sovereign.   Behold, I have narrated all my
story ; for the rest, command and decree are
of His Majesty.' "

"The Khalif was deeply grieved at the mis-
chances of 'Abdu-'llāh, and said to comfort
him, 'Well, now, *if it please God (exalted be
He!),* thy fortune and prosperity are at hand.
Brother, thy kindness and courtesy towards
us are not things to be forgotten.   Although
I sorrow because of the woes that have
befallen thee, still I am glad at having found
a way to repay the favours thou hast shown
me.   First of all, I beg of thee that, no more
slighting the boundless kindness of God for
the sake of Durr-Dāna who has rested thus
long a time in the Abode of Permanency,
thou abandon celibacy and monachism.
There are in my imperial palace damsels a
hundred times more beautiful than she ; I
will show thee all, save only my own concubines, that thou mayest choose one from
among them and be married to her, and
pass a time here in pleasure.   Then will I

send thee with Ja'fer to Basra, and cause thy hidden treasure to be restored to thee.'

" 'Abdu-'llāh was constrained to obey the injunction of the Khalif, and the latter called one of the harem eunuchs and sent word to Her Majesty Zubeyda* to assemble all the slave-girls, save only his own concubines, in such and such a place. When the eunuch returned and informed him that they were ready, Hārūn took 'Abdu-'llāh and they went to the harem. Some three thousand damsels covered with gold and jewels were modestly standing in ranks in a vast hall. Midmost the hall were placed two chairs, on one of which the Khalif sat, and on the other of which 'Abdu-'llāh was permitted to seat himself. All the damsels were ordered to pass one by one before 'Abdu-'llāh. While they were passing, displaying form and figure, and exhibiting dress and deportment, the glance of 'Abdu-'llāh alighted upon one amongst them, and forthwith he swooned and fell

* The chief wife of the Khalif.

from his chair. Crying, 'What has happened?' They flocked around him, and as soon as that damsel looked upon his face she too fainted and fell to the ground. They sprinkled water upon their faces, and when they had brought back their senses the Khalif said to 'Abdu-'llāh, 'What is it?' Scarce able to articulate, he faltered, 'My Sovereign, it is my Durr-Dāna.' Khalif Reshīd, fearing he should die for joy, got him carried out straightway, and when, by causing him to be bled and to take stimulants, he had restored calmness to his heart, Hārūn experienced a delight such as cannot be described.

"Thinking that if they were allowed to meet at once they would both die, he determined that for the first two or three times they should talk to one another and relate their stories from behind a curtain ; so that their fervour might be somewhat cooled. So a curtain was hung up, and they brought Durr-Dāna for 'Abdu-'llāh to converse with, and placed her behind it. The Khalif perceiving

that neither of them was able to commence
the conversation, addressed Durr-Dāna himself, saying, 'I have heard 'Abdu-'llāh's adventures from himself this morning ; but he
said that they cast thee into the Nile ; how
didst thou contrive to escape ?'   'My lord,'
replied she, 'after throwing 'Abdu-'llāh into
the Nile, the executioners conversed among
themselves, saying, "It were better we sold
this poor creature to some foreign slave-
dealer and got a few thousand sequins, than
that we cast her into the water." And after
much consultation, one of them took me and
led me to a ruin, in which he hid me, and
there he threatened me thus : "Be silent ; if
thou utterest a word I will slay thee ;" and
then he departed. He went to a slave-dealer
and, making me out to be a run-away slave-
girl, sold me for two thousand sequins. The
dealer came and made me put on a suit of
men's clothes, and that same day we set out
with a caravan. As he was afraid, he did not
sell me in these parts, but brought me to the

Abode of the Khalifate, where it was my lot
to be sold into your imperial circle.'

"Then 'Abdu-'llāh, gaining courage, began
to speak. After they had once or twice thus
cooled the flame of their ardour by conversing from behind the curtain, they were married and attained all their desires.

"One day, when they had remained for a
month in the palace of the Khalif, attended
with all honour and respect, and in delight,
Hārūn, after a few preliminary words, said
to 'Abdu-'llāh, 'It is my will to make thee
King of Basra.' But 'Abdu-'llāh clasped the
feet of the Khalif, and said, 'My master, if
your imperial clemency see right to grant
my humble request, you will appoint to that
post the cause of my life, Emīr Hayder, son-
in-law of the accursed Elqam ; and that it
may be remorse to his soul during the whole
remainder of his life, you will confirm that
wretch in his office ; and you will kindly re-
instate this your slave in his house as hereto-
fore ; and by these means you will make
him twofold more your slave than he is now.'

"The Khalif granted the request of 'Abdu-
'llāh ; and sent the Vezir Ja'fer with twenty
thousand horsemen to seat Emīr Hayder on
the throne of Basra, and restore 'Abdu-'llāh
safe and well to his house and cavern. After
their arrival Durr - Dāna and 'Abdu-'llāh
passed the rest of their lives together in joy ;
and their story remains in the mouths of
men."

' See now,' said Libāba to Ferah-Naz, ' is
there no constancy in men ?' But Ferah-Naz,
criticising this story, said, ' Mother, lady, this
which you have related cannot be considered
constancy. What kindness or what love had
'Abdu-'llāh experienced from Durr - Dāna
that he should bring himself to the point of
death ? Sincere constancy is brought about
by the acceptance of love ; looked at in this
light, 'Abdu-'llāh's passion was occasioned
by mere fleshly desire, and was patent bru-
tality. Even supposing it were sincere, according to the confession of your own mouth,
when gay with wine he desired to kiss Nā'ila,

daughter of Elqam.   Was not that opposed
to constancy ?   And again, when the Khalif
proposed to give him a slave-girl, was not
his acceptance opposed to constancy ?   If
Durr-Dāna had not appeared among the
damsels, he would surely have accepted
another and married her.   Ah ! no, the constancy of men is not proved by this story ; I
am still in the right.'   For all that Libāba
strove to convince Ferah-Nāz, it was in vain ;
she ever confounded her nurse with clever
refutations and wise demonstrations.

Let us leave them thus, endeavouring to
persuade Ferah-Nāz, and return to Jewād.

CONTINUATION OF THE STORY OF JEWAD.

When Jewād set out from Aleppo, he saw
city after city and town after town, and
acquired information concerning the condition of many peoples.   His road led him to
the city of Cashmere.   As Cashmere was then
the most flourishing and prosperous of all

I

the cities of the East, he determined to pass some time there, and hired a room and occupied himself making acquaintance with the men of learning and culture in the town. All with whom he became acquainted and all with whom he conversed praised and extolled Iklīlu-'l-Mulk, the son of their King, Hurmuz Shah, to such an extent that Jewād conceived an affection for him without having seen him, and sought a pretext for meeting with him.

The Prince, who was only seventeen or eighteen years old, but clever, upright, virtuous, and versed in the general and special sciences, always passed his time conversing with wise masters on sciences and arts. Having heard of the arrival of one of the wandering philosophers, a Bektāshī called Jewād Baba, who was in all manner of knowledge unique in the age, the Prince felt on his part likewise a desire for mutual acquaintance. But as it would not have been courteous to summon at once so eminent a person into his presence, he deemed it best to disguise

himself and go and visit him. So taking two
men along with him, he went to the cell of
Jewād. The latter, as nothing is hidden to
the seer, omitted nought in doing him rever-
ence, and said, 'O my Prince, you have done
me honour, you have raised this your slave
from the dust; but there was no need for
this trouble. Had you sent an order to your
slave, he would have gone to your threshold.'
After such expressions of politeness, they
began to converse, and he bewildered Iklíl
by the extent of his knowledge. When they
had talked for two hours, the Prince bade
Jewād farewell, and requested him to come
to the palace the following day.

When the Prince entered the presence of
his father, he praised Jewād before him to
such a degree that he bewildered him. And
on the following day a horse royally caparisoned and many attendants were sent, and
they brought Jewād with honour. After the
observance of all ceremonies due to kings, he
held a scientific discussion with the Prince,
fair of fortune, before the King and delighted

him. When they had partaken of food, the
King said to Jewād, 'Although by reason of
your leading the life of a qalender, to be in a
royal establishment may be contrary to your
taste, yet it were shame to us that a learned
man like yourself should live in the corner of
a khan; so kindly let them show you a private room in the palace, and reside with us
as our companion.'

Jewād gratefully accepted the offer of the
King, and took up his abode in the palace.
He was never away from the Prince, they
were always together enjoying themselves in
pleasant talk and learned converse. Their
love towards one another rose to such a
degree that each acted as though he were the
other's brother. One day when Hurmuz
Shah was talking alone with Jewād, he said,
'Jewād Baba, I have a secret sorrow; are
you ware of it?' 'No, my lord,' replied the
other, 'pray let me hear.' Then the King
said, 'You know how I have no child save
your adopted brother Iklîl; and that the
desire of children and grandchildren is natural

to fathers and mothers, and especially to
kings. For three years I have wished him to
marry, but he will not consent; he has seen
a vision and his opposition is based thereon;
and though I have striven, it has been in
vain. I beg of your wisdom to undertake
this matter, to prevail upon the Prince to
consent to marry. Only see that he know
not how I have spoken to you about it.'
Jewād replied, 'Most willingly,' and the discussion ended.

Iklíl came to Jewād that night, and while
they were occupied as of wont in conversing
on the sciences, weaving the web of pleasant
words on the frame of speech, the evening
call to worship was chanted. Then said
Jewād to Iklíl jestingly, 'Well, during the day
our profound discussions are all right; but it
will not do to sit on into the night.' 'How
not?' asked the Prince. 'O my lord,' replied
the other, 'the favourites of your harem will
abuse your slave, saying, "A vagabond has
arrived who with his talk keeps our lord from
the harem."' Iklíl smiled and said, 'My lord,

your friend is not married.' Then Jewād
appearing astonished, said, 'Since you know
that it is not conformable to sense and reason
for princes to remain single, why do you
delay?'

With pain and diffidence Iklīl began to
speak on this wise, 'My lord, Jewād Baba,
although I know that I have no power to
reason with you, unique in wisdom, and am
assured that with one word you can refute
all I say, still, if you kindly respect the pro-
verb, "Men speak according to the extent of
their ability," I shall explain to you the cause
of my celibacy. Now, I saw in a vision a
beautiful garden, on the verge of which stood
a fair woman, in the apparel of the daughters
of kings, such that the harem, the imagination, could not contain the bride, her loveliness; far less could she be described. Just
then two deer, a buck and a doe, passed into
the garden; of a sudden the doe was caught
in a trap, and the buck, after a thousand
efforts, brake the snare with his teeth and set
free his mate. Little time elapsed ere the

foot of the buck was likewise entangled in a
snare, and he fell to moaning and crying;
but the doe, heeding not his anguish, abandoned her consort in that plight, and fled
away. Thereupon, I awoke from sleep, and
I knew this to be a celestial warning to me
from the Merciful that I should accept no
wife, even though she wore the form of the
beauty I had beheld. It is this vision which
has made me averse to marriage.'

Jewād smiled and replied, ' My lord, well
known is the story of the sheykh who
preached many days to the folk on the
virtue of liberating purchased slaves, and,
seeing that had no effect, bought a slave himself and set him free, and then saw how great
an effect was produced thereby. Seeing that
I, your slave, am myself a celibate, mayhap
I ought not to advise my lord on this matter;
but I beg of you to give your attention carefully.: It is known unto you, distinguished by
nobility, that " in plurality oneness, and in
oneness plurality " is an axiom agreed upon
among the mystics. The reason of the rules

of the chiefs of the qalenders being that these
poor ones who struggle along the Mystic
Path should wear coarse and tattered garments of this sort and be ill-fed and marry
not (but remain, like Jesus, mateless), is not
merely that, having abandoned attachment
to the world, they may walk lightly in the
Path of Truth ; nay, there is a hidden cause
therefor, within the veil.   If you will deign
to reflect, there are among the Divine favours
and eternal mysteries certain hidden arcana
more adapted for comprehension in this world
of intermediary void, acquaintance with which
is a wondrous grace of the Merciful to the
adepts.   When the pilgrim reaches that land
of knowledge, if he have adopted celibacy
and the drapery of nakedness, it is impossible
that the bonds and affections of the lusts of
humanity should obstruct the road of him,
having staked his all.   For example, if a
qalender hunger, but a few halfpence are
needful for him to repel the pangs of famine;
now, it is a thousand times better to blow the

conch* and collect in the two-beaked alms-
bowl enough of the gifts of Providence to
appease the cravings of hunger than to
trouble over furnace and bellows and crucible
and charcoal and mercury and calx and
alacab and sulphur and tin and arsenic†—
all for a handful of coppers! If the poor
one initiated into these attainable mysteries
called by the names of the Powers of Magic,
Occult Influence, Contraction and Expansion,
the Secret Virtues of Things, and the Divine
Knowledge, be married and have a family,
the cares of children and wife will render
him incapable of bearing the hardships of the
world, and it is clear that he must fall a prey
to slovenliness and vanities, and so lose the
resigned soul in the vale of abandonment.
It is for this weighty reason that the
qalenders who tread the path of poverty and
wander through many lands are restrained
from marrying and having families. Because

---

* Some dervishes make use of a kind of horn.

† *i.e.*, to labour at alchemy.

I am a seeker after strange knowledge and a
newly-started traveller on that path am I
wifeless ; which by the rule of mutual simi-
larity might be worthy of note as an example
for a beggar :* yea, thus is it.   But since celibacy and freedom from care of earthly things
necessarily causes exemption from the pomp
of the world, it is an evident matter that the
opposite thereof is the fitting condition for
kings and kings' sons.   That celibacy is an
obvious error on the part of sovereigns will
appear a self-evident proposition, if you will
deign to consider with the measure of
sagacity.   Philosophers have likened empire
and sovereignty to a bath ; the men outside
of which desire to enter it ; but when they
enter, the warmth of the water afflicts them,
and great weariness comes upon them by
reason of the fierceness of the heat and of the
arising of perspiration and lassitude, so that
full speedily doth their desire to depart
appear.   That the most part of the possessors

* But not for a prince.

of exceeding riches* fancy the severing of the
thread of connection with the rush and crush
of men, and sit with the head hanging on the
collar of the robe of retirement, and somehow choose the corner of privacy, is of the
things proved by the legion of the learned.
But this fancy is unlawful for kings; for
besides it being impossible for them to abandon the pomp of earth, the possession of
their world-swaying minds by this idle notion
is parallel to long-continued relaxation of
the rein of the steed, their royal zeal. Now,
it is not hidden from your imperial far-seeing
sagacity that the only way of preserving the
just constitution of sovereigns from that
deadly poison of the well-being of states, the
nurture of those fancies aforesaid, is that,
bound by the tether of family and offspring
and the solicitude for the circumstances of
their successors and descendants, they should
be devoted to the aim of rendering prosperous their possessions and realms. But putting

* *i.e*, spiritual riches.

those opinions aside, as you have explained
that the only reason of your desire for celibacy is based on the inconstancy of women,
grant that the charger, discourse, may curvet
through that valley too.   My lord, in what
creature or being, in what thing perceived by
the understanding or the senses, nay, in what
in all creation, in the world, in the universe,
in the dwellers therein, in the ages, in the
days and nights, *is* there stability and endurance and unchangeableness and fidelity,
that there should be firmness and constancy
in that seat of human passions called the
heart?   So you must see it becomes not you
or me to talk of constancy; but as the saw
hath it, '*therein is a resemblance with a difference,*' so we shall not say 'constancy,' but 'steadfastness in conduct.'   Now it is manifest that
there is more steadfastness in women than in
men, and it is clear that their character is
superior.   Above all doth the fact that the
submission and fidelity of the wife to the
husband are greater than those of the husband to the wife require no commentary.   A

strange event, which proves all this, occurred
recently in Persia ; deign to give ear, that I
may recount it : '

THE STORY TOLD BY JEWAD TO IKLILU-'L-
MULK.

" It is a strange story and a wondrous tale
which will serve as an example to the ear of
intelligence.   Like as of old time the
supremacy of the 'Abbāsī Khalifs extended
over other sovereigns, so was the rule of the
Kings of Isfahān, who were also the monarchs
of India, China and Persia, acknowledged by
all the potentates of these parts.   A large
body of the inhabitants of El-Bostān presented a petition to the divan of Shābūr
Shah, King of Isfahān, wherein they besought justice and redress against the
oppressions of their King, Ghazanfer Shah,
and announced and declared the extent of
his mercilessness—how every day he walked
the markets and bazaars in different dis-

guises, and paying no attention to Haji or
Khoja, slew the guiltless and innocent ones
engaged in their shops and work-places ; how,
besides slaughtering most of the men, he
broke into the houses of chaste and virtuous
ladies ; and how through his hanging and
killing and shedding the believers' blood, the
half of the inhabitants had perished and the
rest fled on account of their terror—and they
prayed for his dismissal and the appointment
of another, that the People of Muhammed
might be saved.   When he learned this, the
King sent an order by a chamberlain to
Ghazanfer Shah, in which was written : ' On
the arrival of my imperial letter do thou come
hither alone that thou mayest dispute with
thine adversaries : if thou disobey, thy kingdom shall surely be given to another, and
thyself made an example to thy peers ? '

"Ghazanfer sent back the messenger with
the answer that he would start in a little
while ; and three days later he set out alone
for Isfahān, in compliance with the royal
order. He journeyed on till he came to a spot

three hours' distance from Isfahān, where he dismounted at the brink of a fountain a little way off the road. There he thought in himself, ' I am going, imagining that I shall be allowed to explain my circumstances to the King ; but supposing he allow me not to speak, neither grant me leave to declare my hidden sorrow,—were it not a pity to cast myself of my own free will into the gulf of the royal displeasure ?   Rather than do so, it were better to betake me to some place and hide there, and secrete myself in the corner of privacy.   It is probable I shall meet my family some day ; but life is dearer than all.'   When his reflections had led to this conclusion, he saw a flock of sheep on a hillock opposite, which were coming to water where he was.   Determining to go and ask the shepherd what places lay in the various directions, he mounted his horse and ascended the hillock. When he had approached the shepherd, what did he see ?—no shepherd, but one of the youths of Paradise arrayed in shepherd's garb.   As Ghazanfer

had never before seen any of the sons of
Adam so fair of form, he dismounted from
his horse in his bewilderment, and saluted
the shepherd, and stood gazing on his perfect
beauty.   The shepherd, on beholding the
bewilderment of Ghazanfer, asked him, 'Who
are you, and what seek you here?'   He
replied, 'I am a stranger who has met with
a wonderful adventure, and I know not
whither I am going ; but who are you, for it
is clear as the noontide sun that that world-
inflaming beauty is not the beauty of a shepherd ?'   'Sit down that we may converse a
little,' said the other ; and they seated themselves in the shade of a tree.   Then said the
shepherd to Ghazanfer, 'Until thou hast told
me the truth concerning thine adventures, I
will not tell thee who I am.'   So Ghazanfer,
concealing nothing, related how he was the
King of El-Bostān, how he had come in con-
sequence of being summoned, and how he
had changed his intention on that spot and
resolved on flight.   Then the shepherd said,
'Ah ! beware, rely not on them, rush not of

thine own accord into the abyss of death ;
the present king is not the former king ; too
late repentance profits not.' After much
advice to Ghazanfer, the shepherd began the
narration and thus explained the mystery :—

THE STORY OF SHABUR AND HUMA.

" 'I am Humā, daughter of Gushtesp Khan
the sovereign of Tūrān. I grew up amidst
tenderness and pleasure till I reached my
fifteenth year ; when one night, having occasion to go out, I took a candle in my hand,
and, without wakening the slave-girls, went
forth. When I came back I left the door
open. I had a favourite cat which, having
got in, came in beside me, and playing about,
put me off my sleep. I had placed my
bracelets which I had taken off in the evening
upon the mattress, and while I was watching
the gambols of the cat, it seized one of them
in its mouth and fled out of the room.
Fearing it would drop it somewhere, I ran
after it and tried to catch it, but it escaped

K

and rushed down the stair into the cellar. When I reached the cellar-door in pursuit of it, I saw a light within the cellar; thinking it was one of the slave-girls who had gone in there for some purpose, I fearlessly descended the stair and went in. I beheld no cellar, but a room regally furnished, in the place of honour of which sat a lovely youth of seventeen or eighteen years of age. My senses fled away and I sought to return, but there was no door at the place where I had entered; and I looked in bewilderment towards the youth. He too gazed at me in perfect confusion. When I asked him, 'Who are you, and what kind of place is this?' he replied, 'Who are you, and what kind of place is this?' and I was bereft of my senses. He, conceiving me to be a princess, said, 'My Life! I am Shábúr, son of Gúdarz Sháh, the King of Isfahán. Two minutes ago I opened the door of the ante-chamber of our own house, and was entering the harem, when I found myself here; is not this your house?' 'Yes,' I answered, 'it is our house; but there is no subterranean room

like this in our house. The truth is that the
cat ran off with my bracelet, and I went into
the cellar to catch it, when I beheld thee and
this room; but I cannot now find the door
by which I entered.' He said, 'Oh! thou
didst not enter by a door; thou descendest
through the ceiling. Come, damsel, sit down,
what is all this?'

"After he had looked at me and I had
looked at him for a time, the Prince, gathering courage, said, 'Since thou art neither
jinn nor fairy; but like myself hast met with
some strange hap, come, rise, let us go out
and see what manner of place this is.' So
we both went out of the room together; and
we saw a lofty hall in the centre whereof was
a curiously wrought chandelier of crystal with
about fifty lighted candles. There were
some thirty or forty doors round the hall;
we pulled aside a little the curtain which
hung in front of one of these and peeped in
—a beautiful youth and damsel were lying
together on a couch. We looked into another, and saw just as in the former a lovely

youth and damsel asleep. We examined
other rooms, and in each we found as before
a pair of beauties.   In the eleventh were
seated a youth and lady conversing in a
world of their own.   We made bold and
entered. When they saw us they smiled
and said, ' Have you come at last?' and,
showing great delight, they arose and wel-
comed us. The youth whom we found in
the room then said with smiles, ' *What things
God wills!* do not these suit each other
beautifully?   Banish your dismay, there is
nought to fear.'   They made us sit down,
and that youth said joyously to our youth,
' My lord, your slave is Monla Idrīs, son of
the Sultan Monla Yezīd; so I am your
brother, being likewise a prince. And this
my companion is the daughter of Sultan
Imānu-'d-Dīn the Tubba' of Yemen, just as
that pure one by your side is the child of
some Sultan.   We, both of us, in one day, in
one moment, met with an adventure similar
to that which has befallen you, and found
ourselves here. You may ask how we know

you to be the children of kings ; well, in
each of these rooms is there a prince and a
king's daughter. This vast place is the
palace of a crafty sorceress ; however, no
treatment but kindness and attention is
observed towards any of us by her ; once a
week she comes and jests and plays with us
and counsels us to employ ourselves with
pleasure and delight. She has appointed
special attendants to observe and gratify our
every fancy, whatever it may be, in the
manner we may wish ; indeed, all those appliances of joy which, while under the shade
of our fathers we could not obtain, are here
lavished upon us without stint, agreeably to
each one's due. Thus is it that henceforth
we hope no more to see our parents ; for this
unbeliever ever tells us that her object in
bringing hither the sons and daughters of
kings is that, the race of monarchs being cut
off, anarchy and confusion may fill the world ;
and she gives us friendly counsel, saying,
'There is no escape hence for you till the
Resurrection, vex not your hearts with the

thought thereof.' See, after this explanation nothing remains for you to fret about ; now go to your room, there is a clean bed in the press, spread it out, and occupy yourselves with pleasure, with hearts at ease. In the morning you will meet with the other brethren, and all anxiety will disappear.' So saying, they sent us back to our room, where each of us in a separate corner, while musing and marvelling, was overcome by sleep.

"'We woke when it was morning, and five or six beautiful slave-girls came in and brought us breakfast and coffee and tobacco, and waited on us. In a little while, couple by couple, entered some thirty princes and kings' daughters, and they assembled in our room. After performing the ceremony of greeting, they proceeded to comfort us, each telling of what king he or she had been the darling, and in what manner he or she appeared to have come there. Just then a slave-girl brought in a chair, and saying, 'The lady is coming,' placed it in the middle of the room. I saw a corpulent woman of

about sixty years of age come in, who said,
' Hail, my sons, my parrots.'* After she had
treated them all with kindness and favour,
she called for us, asking with great respect,
' Where are the Kings' children who arrived
last night?' When she had flattered and
caressed us, she said to the others, ' Now, my
darlings, do you rise and go to your rooms,
that I may marry these.' Having sent them
all away, she smiled on us and said, ' See,
now, you are husband and wife; henceforward do you ever occupy yourselves with
pleasure; if either of you oppose the other, we
shall quarrel.' Having said this she retired ;
and when we were left alone, scarce knowing
what I did, I ran and fell at the Prince's feet
and cried, ' Mercy, my lord, for the sake of
God and the Prophet have compassion upon
me,·and deface not the honour of me forlorn!'
Weeping, the Prince replied, 'Be at peace ; I
am not of the men you fear ; I knew from
your conduct of last evening that you were

* *i.e.*, My fair girls.

virtuous and chaste.   May the Most High
Creator preserve us from committing acts
forbidden.   Amen !   No other occupations
than adoration and entreaty of the All-Per-
former and worship of the Deliverer befit
thee and me in a strait like this.   Now, let
us unite our hearts, and, as much as in us
lies, wait at the Door of the Divine Power,
where answers are accorded.   God Almighty
is able to save us.   But if we commit vile
crimes like these shameless ones whom we
have seen, no portion shall be ours in the
world or the Hereafter but ruin and despair.
If it please God (exalted be He) that we be
delivered from this misfortune, we shall be
wedded and married conformably to the
Divine ordinance ; but if escape be impossible
and we die, our hope is that we may be
united for ever in the bowers of Paradise.'

"'When he said this I was rejoiced as
though the world were my own, and I wept
with a loud voice and clasped the Prince's
feet.   We were delighted at the concord of
our hearts and forgot our sorrows, and, having

recited the Fātiha* over our agreement, occupied ourselves worshipping the Deliverer
in sincerity. Thus we continued to act
without giving the others any idea thereof;
and we shut the doors of the room as though
we were employed like themselves, and all
the while we were engaged in uninterrupted
devotions, worshipping the Saver. When
forty days had thus passed and the number
of prayers had reached forty thousand, and
we, having found an opportunity at noon,
had recommenced the recitation, that vile
sorceress fell of a sudden a victim to the
invincible sword of the All-Compeller, and
her wicked soul was consigned to the fire of
hell. And the slave-girls began to cry out,
' The old lady is dead !' Just then there was
a great earthquake and a frightful roar, and
a black smoke filled the domes of the palace,
and it grew so dark that we could not see
one the other. For a quarter of an hour the

---

* The First Chapter of the Qur'ān, recited over all com-
pacts, and upon other occasions of importance.

smoke grew denser, when suddenly in a
second it cleared away : when what did I
see ?—I was in my own room in my father's
palace in Tūrān.

" ' When I saw my slave-girls I was
amazed, and they screamed and ran to my
father and mother, and told them of my
reappearance in my room. They both came
and fell upon me, and, weeping much, asked
about my absence and appearance. I told
them the whole of my adventures, and besought my father to send a man to Isfahān
to ascertain if the Prince had likewise been
delivered. So my father despatched a special
chamberlain to the King of Isfahān with
some presents, and a note setting forth my
strange experiences, and enquiring concerning the lot of the Prince. But that mine of
constancy, the Prince Shābūr, had also sent
a man to my father to enquire about my
fate ; and the two letter-bearers met half-
way. When they had communicated one
with the other, and discovered that the object
of both parties was the same, they compared

the letters and saw that the King of Isfahān's
note contained these words additional : 'in
the time of their tribulation your daughter
Humā promised to wed my Prince Shābūr,
conformably to the Divine ordinance ; if she
remain faithful to her plight, I shall send
men to fetch her hither to be married.' As
this question required an answer, our messenger returned with the Isfahān officer.
Whenever the request was made known to
my father, he asked me, and, having seen
my desire, sent off an envoy with the answer
that all were agreeable.

"'But let us not be prolix ; in a little
while came the Vezir as the Prince's repre-
sentative, and some of the women and
eunuchs of the harem to keep us company,
and more than ten thousand soldiers to
guard us on the way, and they took us off
to Isfahān. I was married to Prince Shābūr;
and so our desires were fulfilled on earth by
the union we had imagined deferred till
heaven. Two years afterwards my father-in-

law, Gūdurz Shah, was received into mercy ; and Shābūr sat upon his throne.

"'We lived for five years with perfect love and great devotion towards one another, so much so that we could not endure to be parted even for a single hour. Fifteen days ago I undressed the King in the evening and laid him in his bed, and then went myself into a room near the bed-chamber to perform the evening worship. Having completed it, I put on my night-clothes and returned to the King, when I beheld someone lying in his arms. 'Who is that?' I cried ; and the King and she who was in his embrace turned round and looked in his face ; I too looked with attention, and saw the woman clasping the King ; and the King and I, and she who resembled me, we all three of us, stared amazed and bewildered, one at the other. Then the King addressed me, saying, 'Who art thou that comest thus untimely in the form of my wife and frightenest us?' My senses fled from me and I began to weep, and said, 'My lord, thy wife Humā ; what is

that phantom by thy side? for the love of
God look attentively at me!' Then the
other said, 'That wretch who has appeared
will drive us mad; call the slave-girls on
guard that they may turn her away;' and
again she clung to the neck of the King and
wept. The King clapped his hands, and
the slave-girls on guard entered, and they
marvelled at seeing me doubled, and at
hearing the dispute between us. The King,
who was intelligent, remembered that I had
a mole upon my body; he looked at the
same part of the person of the phantom by
his side, and saw the mole was there; then
he told me to open my dress, and as I knew
that his object was to see that mole, I opened
it. When he saw the mole upon me likewise,
he was confounded and called for my nurse.
On coming in, the poor old woman began to
cry aloud at seeing Humā in two cages; *
but the King called out to her, 'Cease thy

---

* There is a play here upon the word Humā, which is the
name of a fabulous bird; the two cages being the two
bodies,—the Queen and the phantom.

weeping, and take her who is standing there
aside, and ask her concerning the events of
her childhood, by that means thou mayst
discover which is the true.' So my nurse
took me apart, and put to me certain questions about some things that had happened
in my childhood, all of which I truthfully
answered. When she had likewise ques-
tioned the other in private, and received full
and correct answers, my nurse cried out,
'My lord, each of those is without doubt
Humā.' The King was sore distressed ;
and when he had himself asked me about
certain private things which had happened
between us, and interrogated the other, he
saw that there was not a hair's difference
betwixt her and me. He took council, and
said to my nurse, 'One of these must necessarily be a phantom, and is to us some sort
of delusion ; and what seems self-evident is
this, that the one which came afterwards,
while I was with my wife, is the false one ;
send it away, but use no violence ; begone !'
and he motioned me away. Although I

implored it was of no avail, and my own nurse took me by the hand and thrust me without the gate, and crying, 'Begone, vile wretch!' drove me forth. Knowing not where to go, weeping I wandered on in the middle of the night through the wards of the city, till I passed beyond its bounds. The Lord Most High protected me from interference of evil men; and without the city I met a shepherd ninety years of age, who was tending his sheep. I went up to him, but he was so old that he could not discern that I was a woman. He treated me with kindness, and I went with him to his fold, and took refuge with him; and for fifteen days have I been in that old man's service."

"Ghazanfer marvelled at the adventures of Humā, and she wept in silence thinking of her lot. After much reflection Ghazanfer addressed her thus, 'From this story of thine it is evident that thou wilt never be able to make thyself known hereafter; come then with me and be my companion and let us off

to another land.' Humā smiled sadly and
said, 'Brother is the object of flight escape
from the condition of a shepherd? Know
this for certain, that I would not exchange
this condition of shepherd in which I can see
from afar the city where dwells my King for
the empire of the world ; this is a trial to me
from the Merciful, and it is known unto the
wise that patience is the only resource in trial.'

"Whilst they were thus talking, a man
mounted on a chestnut horse appeared coming at full speed from the direction of the
fountain ; he rushed up the hillock and
passed by them like the blinding lightning.
He was a young man, seemingly of twenty-
two or twenty-three years, elegantly dressed,
and his horse was richly caparisoned. When
Humā beheld his face she exclaimed, ' Lo, it
is King Shābūr ! ' Just then appeared another man upon a grey horse, with a sword
in his hand advancing with furious speed
and excitement ; when he passed they saw
him to be identical with the former, in appearance he too was King Shābūr. Humā

cried out, 'Mercy! what form is that? they
are both my lord!' Ghazanfer, who was a
bold and valiant man, unable to brook this,
straightway mounted his steed and pursued
them at full speed. He overtook the Sultan
with the sword, who, on seeing him, cried, 'O
brother, seize yon wretch!' and besought his
aid. As Ghazanfer's horse was in good condition, he came up with the fellow, and,
without allowing him to speak, struck him on
the head with his mace and hurled him to
the ground. The King too came up and
waved his sword over him, when the fellow
exclaimed, 'Mercy! hold, kill me not, that I
may tell thee who I am.' And he drew from
his finger a ring, like the ring of the door of
the Ka'ba,* and thereupon he became a
white-bearded old man of sixty. He fell to
begging forgiveness and crying, 'Mercy! my
King, pardon my crime;' and Shābūr Shāh
and Ghazanfer were amazed, and on their
questioning him, he thus explained :

* The Sacred Temple at Mekka.

L

"'The woman now in your palace, whom you think to be your wife, was in the time of her youth a harlot. She had very many gallants, of whom I was one; but as she loved me beyond the rest, she one day said to me, "Thou knowest that I have a thousand lovers, none of whom I may renounce, but thou art dearer to me than all; if thou desire it, marry me that thou mayest freely enter and leave my house, but thou must agree to molest none of the gallants." I consented to this arrangement and married her. For a long time we lived in the shade of the gallants, but the woman grew old and her trade left her, and no one would look at her; and we became anxious for the necessities of life. One day the woman said to me, "Husband, we have no remedy left us save this: there is in a certain city a skilful sorceress whom I have known for long. If we enter her service I think it will be the means of obtaining our livelihood with ease." I agreed to this proposal, and we went to the city where the sorceress lived. When she saw us she was

greatly delighted, and she entertained us
with kindness for a month. At the end of
that time she said, " Since you have come
seeking me, I shall make you a gift such that
you may be free from penury for ever." She
then performed a disgusting magic ceremony
by which she produced two silver rings, one
of which she gave to me and the other to the
woman. And she said, " Lo, take these, and
when you desire to be changed into the form
of any of the great or rich, put your ring
upon your finger, and that moment you shall
assume the appearance and become acquainted with the position, ideas, and knowledge of him whom you select,—that is, you
shall become his double ; prosper in your
undertakings." And she sent us away. We,
husband and wife, consulted and agreed that
it were better to assume the forms of a king
and queen, and pass the rest of our lives in
sovereignty, than to choose those of any
meaner persons. So fifteen days ago the
woman came to your couch in the form of
Humā and deceived you, and made you

drive away your real wife. To-day I, too,
took your form, but have failed to succeed.
Thus is it. If you will have pity because my
crime is by reason of the greatness of my
poverty, compassion is yours ; if you pity not
but slay, I am in your hands.'

"Shābūr Shah said to Ghazanfer, 'What
sayest thou? look at the crime of this
wretch, and look at his request for pardon.'
'My lord,' replied he, 'I have good news for
you, as a thank-offering perchance you may
incline to forgiveness.' And he told him
how Humā, in the dress of a shepherd, was
waiting under the tree. 'Well,' said King
Shābūr, 'take the fellow and come ;' and he
took the ring himself and went to the place
where Humā was. When the latter saw the
King she fell down before him and they
wept much together, and Shābūr Shah thus
related, 'To-day I desired to go out in disguise, and, having put on other clothes, went
out by the palace gate, when I recollected
that I had forgotten something which I had
to say to Humā. As it was a private matter,

I could not send a message by anyone, so I turned back and entered the harem, when I saw a fellow exactly like myself sitting with Humā. I straightway drew my sword, and he fled and mounted upon my horse that was harnessed, and took to flight; I leapt upon another horse and pursued him to this spot ; lo, the rest has been seen of yourselves.'

"Ghazanfer brought the horse which the fellow had ridden, and covering Humā with a shawl, seated her upon it. He and the King mounted also, and, having made fast the man's hands, leading him after them, they proceeded quietly to the city. The King, attending not to Humā's alighting, hastened to the harem, and came up to the side of the wretch who wore the Queen's form. She, imagining him to be her own husband, said, ' Hast thou won to kill him ? ' ' Out on thee, vile unbeliever, take the ring from off thy finger,' cried the King. The woman, perceiving that the secret was discovered, and that he who had arrived was

not her husband, but Shābūr Shah, unable
to find any escape, pulled off the ring which
was on her finger, and she became a vile and
hideous old hag. The King took the ring
from her hand also, and, crying, 'Take this
wretch and shut her up somewhere,' went
out. They brought Humā into the harem
in her shepherd's dress, and, after she had
resumed her proper attire, her nurse and all
the slave-girls came and kissed the ground
at her feet.

" Next day the grandees of the empire
were assembled, and the old man and woman
were summoned, and along with them the
witness of all that had happened, Ghazanfer,
who was as yet unknown to the King and
court.   When the King had related the
events, all were silent ; and, out of gratitude
for re-union with Humā, he refrained from
the shedding of blood, and ordered his Vezir
to banish the sorcerers to a distant city.

" After that he called Ghazanfer to his side
and said, 'Brother, thou art the cause of my

life. Art thou Khizr?* who art thou?'
'My master,' replied he, 'I am your slave,
Ghazanfer, King of El-Bostān, whom you
did summon to a dispute.' Then the King
manifested great delight and said, 'Thine
aiding us in our time of need is a sufficient
proof of the goodness of thy nature, and that
the rumours concerning thee are calumnies.'
'Nay, my sovereign,' answered Ghazanfer,
'your slave would not that the people should
say concerning my lord the King, "Ghazanfer, having done somewhat at the Capital,
has been acquitted; the King heeds not the
rights of his poor subjects." In very deed
their complaint was not a lie or a calumny.
I am constrained to speak the truth in your
imperial presence; but there are some of
those grandees standing before you for
whom it is unlawful to hear my poor story.'
'If thou desire,' said Shābūr Shah, 'they all
shall leave, and when the room is emptied

---

* A mysterious personage who comes to the aid of
Muslims in distress.

thou mayest relate.' 'No, my sovereign,' replied Ghazanfer, 'it is very necessary that the others hear.' The King asked which of them he wished sent away, so he pointed out six of the vezirs and ministers. As among them was one, a favourite of the King, the latter thought in himself, 'Surely he imagines that these have received bribes from the people that he wants them dismissed.' So he asked Ghazanfer, 'Dost thou know who the persons are whom thou hast made to be turned out of the room?' And he answered, 'No, my sovereign, never in the course of our lives have I seen them or have they seen me; and now I know not even their names or their offices; but when I have finished my adventures, the reason of their dismissal will be known to your Majesty.' And he thus began to disclose his secrets and relate his wondrous story:

THE STORY OF GHAZANFER AND RAHILA.

"'I am the son of a wealthy merchant of Shīrāz, Zeynu-'d-Dīn by name, and am descended through my father from the Imām Ja'fer Sādiq.* In my childhood I went for instruction to a school, at which attended a damsel named Rāhila, six or seven years old, the daughter of a person named Qadi Huseyn, one of the descendants of 'Alī through El-Hanefiyya.† We learned the alphabet at the desk of the same usher, and grew fond of each other after the way of children; and on holidays I would sometimes go to their house, and she would sometimes come to ours to play. As we grew older our attachment to one another increased till human passion pointed us to " figurative love, the bridge to Truth ;"‡ and we pledged each the other to become husband and wife. When Rāhila reached her tenth year she left the school, and they hid her sweet beauty

* The sixth of the Imāms, descendants of 'Alī, revered by the Shī'a sect.

† The second wife of 'Alī.

‡ The affection of lovers or of husband and wife has been called " figurative love," as held to shadow forth love for God, which is Truth.

from me. Two years after this separation,
my parents, having learned of the tie between
Rāhila and myself, askcd her in marriage for
me from her father. He made no objection,
so we were married according to the Divine
ordinance; and for fourteen years with perfect love we acted towards one another as
husband and wife, without fault on either
side.

"'One Sacrificial-Feast-day, having performed the festival worship, I went straight
to my house; but Rāhila had fallen asleep,
waiting for me. Seeing her asleep, I thought
to frighten her by way of jest, and threw myself upon her, when the dagger which was in
my sash fell from its sheath, and penetrated
to her vitals and came out at her back, nail-
ing her to the board. As I saw that Rāhila
did not awake, I rose from her and I beheld
the dagger which was in my sash plunged
up to the hilt in the body of my beloved, and
I fell down in a swoon.

"'In the course of an hour my senses returned and I thought in myself, "What has

happened ? I have slain my darling, my
soul cannot endure to look no more upon the
beauty of Rāhila," and without telling anyone in the house, I went out. While I was
going along I saw an old man standing at
a door, who, on perceiving me, cried out,
"My son, my master, come in ;" and he took
me by the hand and led me into his house
and shut the door. He gave me a chair and
treated me with kindness and courtesy, and
said, " Son, thy passing is a mercy ; my child
'Abdu-'l-Mālik has gone somewhere, apparently one of our brethren has got hold of him
to assist him ; but there is no difference
between thee and him ; kill these sheep according to our rites ; see, there are the four
sheep, this big one is 'Alī, the son of Abū-
Tālib, this one is Fātima, this is Hasan, and
this Huseyn."* And over each of them he
repeated opprobrious expressions—*God (exalted be He!) guard us!*—the very hearing

---

* Fātima is the daughter of the Prophet and wife of 'Alī,
Hasan and Huseyn are their sons, all are sacred with the
Shī'a sect which prevails in Persia.

of which were a sufficient cause for the wrath
of the Creator and reason for the ire of the
Almighty. On my perceiving that he was a
despiser of the House of the Apostolate, the
vein of Hāshimī* zeal throbbed in my heart
and I cried, " Where is the knife ? " " Here,
my son," he replied, " I sharpened it with
my own hand," and he handed me a large
knife.   I seized it, and crying " *God is most
great !*" struck with all my might at the neck
of the old man, so that he knew not in what
manner his vile soul was consigned to the
flames of hell.

" ' The horse of the slain heretic was ready
saddled, so I mounted it and went forth the
city, and fled to the mountains and wilds.
After wandering for two months I happened
upon El-Bostān, where, hiring a room in one
of the caravanserays, I dwelt for five months
with my griefs and woes. One of the inmates
of the khan who used sometimes to come to

---

* Hāshim is the great-grandfather of the Prophet, whose
descendant Ghazanfer was through Fātima.

my room and keep me company, imagining
that my ceaseless melancholy arose from my
lack of worldly goods, addressed me thus,
"Brother, God is gracious, this much dejection is not lawful, God is gracious ; I have a
fellow-townsman at the royal court, to whom
I spoke of thee, and he told me to bring thee
to him for that he would find thee a fitting
office. If it be thy desire, come, let us go."
"Very well," said I, "we shall see what will
be the favour of God in this matter ;" and
we went together to the palace.

"'Now he whom that man had spoken of
as his fellow-townsman was the King's sherbet-server ; and I advanced and kissed his
skirt, and he asked my name and country.
I answered all, and he, perceiving my intelligence from my manner and replies, requested
the officer of the palace who held the position
of sword-bearer to appoint me assistant to
the sherbet-server ; and so he got me entered
on the roll of the King's servants. As I held
up the curtain while sherbet and coffee were
being served, I was constantly in the presence

of the King. The King, who was a fair prince
called Rizā Qūlī Khan, was pleased with my
manners and appearance, and from time to
time he addressed me with kindness, and he
honoured me and favoured me till I became
of those who approached near unto him. I
loved the King, and his goodness made me
forget my sorrow ; I was of his favourite
attendants, and I rose step by step till I
became page of the key.*

"'One day, six years after my entrance
into the King's establishment, I went out into
the garden alone, and having performed the
afternoon-worship, I sat down in the shade
of a tree and thought of Rāhila and wept till
slumber overcame me, and I slept.   It was
evening, near the time for retiring ; now the
harem of the King had received permission
to go into the garden to see some fireworks,
and the place had been cleared of men ; but
as it was near night some of the ladies had
gone in, when I heard a sound as of running

* An officer of trust in the houses of great men.

while I yet slept, and I awoke. What did I
behold?—it was night, and a lovely damsel
stood before me in the moonlight gazing into
my face. When I looked at her I saw her
to be a woman differing not one hair's tip
from Rāhila. Seeing me greatly bewildered,
she asked, "Who art thou?" I told her that
I was page of the key, and that while I was
walking about the garden sleep had overcome me; and I asked her who she was.—
She told me that she was 'Ayn-i Wefā, one
of the favourites of the king ; then I implored
her to let me escape ere any of the other
damsels should see me. "Well done, master,
and then thou wilt go and say that thou hast
seen me ; that shall not be." And she came
and sat down beside me and cried out,
" Come damsels, see what God has given
me ; " and about a hundred damsels, her
mates, flocked round her, and she showed
me to them all. Then she led me to a
room ; unable to resist, I acquiesced, for by
reason of the greatness of her resemblance
to Rāhila I was infatuated by her, and no

apprehension came into my mind. We
amused ourselves with music and other
diversions till morning, when she sent me
out, begging me to be in the same spot
again on a certain night. When I left I
went to my own room, and, recalling the
image of Rāhila, I would now tear my collar
through grief at the thought that it was
treachery towards her I was practising, and
now be overcome of the beauty of 'Ayn-i Wefā
—through my love and affection for Rāhila.

"'However, when the promised night
arrived, I went with the greatest eagerness
to the appointed place. One of the damsels
was waiting for me: she took me and brought
me to the same room as before. When
'Ayn-i Wefā saw me she ran to welcome me,
and led me in and seated me in the place
of honour; and we diverted ourselves with
music and all sorts of amusements. Now, it
was six years since this 'Ayn-i Wefā had
been procured, and the King, pleased with
her beauty, had entered her among his wives
and sought to marry her. But she had

shown no liking for the King, and he, out of
the greatness of his love, had deemed it unbecoming to use any manner of force ; and,
thinking that she would become reconciled
by kindness, had ordered all the damsels
nowise to oppose her in anything she should
wish. But the ignoring and tolerating of
conduct such as this being altogether impossible, one of the harem eunuchs who had
observed us on the first occasion told it to
the King. The latter, not having believed
his mere word, was waiting for some way of
making sure when the same eunuch informed
him that the page of the key was again in
the harem. As for us, we were playing and
laughing and crying out when the King
entered the room, shouting, ' O cursed
wretch !' 'Ayn-i Wefa sprang forward and
seized the King's hand with extreme delight,
and said, ' Hold, my King, no manner of
anger ever becomes kings until they are
aware of the true condition of its object ;
now, rest a little, sit down and learn about
us ; afterwards no one may oppose our lord's

M

ire, should he still retain it.' And she made
the King sit down and kissed his feet and
said, ' My King, this is not a man to do any
wrong. Your handmaid intended that they
should go and tell our lord, and that he
should discover us thus engaged, that so she
might find a way to unfold her wish. Be
gracious, and drive away the urgings of
anger; be tranquil, and listen for a little
while to the adventures of your handmaid.'
When she had thus cooled the wrath of the
King, he said to her, 'Speak and we shall
see;' and I was standing aside, trembling
with shame and terror.

" ''Ayn-i Wefā thus commenced, 'My lord,
my original name is Rāhila, and I am at this
moment the wedded wife of yon Ghazanfer.'
When I heard her say this, the bird, my soul,
well-nigh escaped from the cage, my body;
for I swooned and fell senseless on the
ground. 'What is this!' cried the King,
'here there must be some strange mystery;'
and he himself arose, and sprinkling water
on my face, revived me. However it may be,

the moment I recovered, unrestrained and undaunted by the presence of the King, I threw my arms round Rāhila's neck, and again fainted. The King, out of the greatness of his kindness, comforted me, saying, 'Gently, son, we will arrange the matter ;' and he made Rāhila and myself sit down. As he enquired about the circumstances from the beginning, Rāhila told him our story from its commencement ; and thus did she detail what happened after she had been killed :

"'When the bird, my soul, flew from the cage, my body, I found myself in a wondrous place, the description whereof were impossible. Ere a moment had elapsed an unseen voice called to me, 'Daughter someone seeketh thee without ;' and straightway I moved from my place to go forth. I raised my eyes, and there was standing before me a glorious personage, just of stature and most sweet of face, and I saw that in his hand was a blood-stained dagger. No fear came upon me from his presence, and I asked, 'Who are you, and what seek you

here?' He answered, 'Fear not, my daughter, I am 'Alī, the son of the uncle of the
Prophet, the consort of the Virgin.*   Thy
husband, Ghazanfer, thought to sport with
thee, when his dagger (which is this dagger)
fell from its sheath, and he slew thee unwit-
tingly.   He fled, and while on the way an
infidel, of the enemies of our family, thinking
him to be of his own people, took him into
his house to perform a wicked deed.   When
Ghazanfer had made sure that the infidel was
of our enemies, crying, "*God is most great!*"
he slew him.   By the permission of God, the
Mighty, the sound of his shout reached my
ears, and I am sent to restore thee to life.'
When he had said this, I kissed the dust at
his feet and asked, 'In what plight is Ghazanfer now?'   He answered, 'Rise and put
on this suit of men's clothes and go forth and
thou shalt find him.   And when thou hast
found him salute him from me and say that
in these days one of the vile marks and signs

* Fātima, the daughter of the Prophet.

of which the enemies of the Apostolic House &
make use, in order to recognise each other, is
a counterfeit mole. There is on the neck of
Ghazanfer a mole of the creation of God, and
that slaughtered infidel by reason of his age
could not distinguish that it was not counterfeit, so, imagining him to be of his own
people, he revealed to him his secret. Tell
thou him that henceforward he is commis-
sioned from God to slay all those upon whom
he may see that mole.'

" 'When he had said this he vanished from
beside me. My King, *Glory to God!* ever
from the time that the Blessed 'Alī said to
me, 'Fear not,' has all dismay passed from
my heart ; so I dreaded not you, and the
reason of my not seeking my enfranchise-
ment by the relation of my adventures was
my being without fear. Conformably to the
command, I put on the men's clothes and
went forth. Somehow, from my manners
and movements they knew me for a woman
in the city of the Moguls ; and the officer,

taking me to be a run-away slave-girl, arrested me and sent me to my King.'

"When she had finished speaking, the King arose from his seat and said, 'And have those eyes seen our Lord 'Alī?' And he kissed Rāhila between the eyes and myself upon the forehead. And he said to me, 'Sit here and condole with Rāhila;' and to the slave-girls, 'These are your master and mistress,—serve ye them;' and he left and went to his own apartments. I leave the estimating of the happiness and value of that night to the heart that has yearned. When it was morning the King returned to the room where we were, and said to me with great respect, 'Come, my life, my son;' and he took me by the hand and led me to the court of the divan. The grandees of the empire were present at the divan, and he addressed them thus: 'Of my own free choice and will I have resigned to this my son Ghazanfer the crown and throne which I inherited from my ancestors.' And he motioned me to sit upon the throne. I resisted

not, but sat upon it. The King was the first
to swear allegiance to me, and he whispered
in my ear, 'My son, show no negligence in
the matter of the holy-warfare to which thou
hast been called;' and he then retired to his
private abode. Since that day I have been
King of El-Bostān; and, having myself
sought out all the cruel wretches in those
parts, have severed their accursed veins, and
cleansed that land of them. Lo, my King,
that is the reason of my shedding of blood.
And it is because that mark is upon them
that I turned these villains from your
presence.'

"The hearts of all present melted within
them, and King Shābūr ordered the imme-
diate execution of the men who had been
turned out, and then kissed Ghazanfer on the
forehead, and thus commanded him, 'Search
likewise Isfahān, and slay all those upon
whom thou seest the mark of sin, and when
thou hast cleansed these parts from the filth

of the Yezīds,* go back to the government of
El-Bostān.' He willingly consented to slay
the Yezīds who were in the imperial city,
but as he begged that El-Bostān should be
again conferred on Rizā Qūlī Khan, and
that he himself should be allowed to rest
with Rāhila in the shade of the King, El-
Bostān was given as before to Rizā Qūlī,
and, having completed the holy-warfare by
the total annihilation of the hypocrites in
Isfahān, Ghazanfer brought thither Rāhila
with every honour; and they remained in
the capital for the rest of their lives."

When Jewād had finished this story, by
the moral of which he hoped to induce
Iklīlu-'l-Mulk to marry, the latter said doubt-
fully, 'It is good, my master, but how can it
be known that a lady of honour and constancy such as Rāhila is to be found?'

---

* Yezīd was son of Mu'āviyya, and second Khalif of the
House of 'Umeyya.   He brought about the murder of
Hasan and Huseyn, the sons of 'Alī, and is never mentioned by the Shī'a sect without execration.   His name is
here used as a term of abuse.

Jewād replied, 'My Prince, in very truth
your objection is worthy of attention ; the
universe is comprehended of the knowledge
of the Divine Majesty ; but not a creature
knows in what condition the fickle human
heart may next moment be ; in sooth, no
person knows his own self, how then could
he be known of another? It cannot be right
for anyone to exceed in this matter and
pledge himself for the conduct of another,
that I should urge my lord, pointing out and
describing a certain damsel and saying, 'there
is of the chaste beauties of such and such a
place a lady of constancy of such and such a
character.' But the Divine Knowledge can
not be gainsaid. *If it please God (exalted be
He!)* we shall go to-morrow for a stroll to a
quiet spot without the city ; and if I can
convince you, you will yield.' Having said
this, they left talking, and the Prince retired
and Jewād lay down in a world of his own.

When it was morning the Prince mounted
with two of his confidential pages, and, having
placed Jewād upon a royal horse, they went

forth of the city to an oratory called 'the
Pilgrims' Seat.' They sat down in the shade
of a tent which was erected, and, after partaking of coffee, Jewād dismissed the pages,
telling them to return to the city and come
back in an hour. When they were left alone
he said, 'My Prince, the reason of my causing
thee to perform this act of power (and thus
disclosing a mystery) is to convince thee; but
thou must promise me never again to do the
deed I am about to teach thee.' Having
made Iklīl swear many oaths, he drew forth
a piece of paper, a reed-pen, and an inkhorn,
and gave them to the Prince; he then showed
him how to construct a five-square charm
vacant in the centre. Thus, according to the
rule of the aërial figure, he made Iklīl commence at the beginning with the number 18,
and complete the igneous houses by the addition of 4 to the number in each, and then
subtract 51 from the total. Next he caused
him to write in the middle house the name
of the Spiritual Minister resulting from this
calculation, cut off the edges of the paper,

and lay down the charm ; then he instructed
him to repeat the Spiritual Name as many
times as the total of the numbers on one side.
When the repetitions of the Spiritual Name
had reached the number of the total amount
of the figures on one side of the charm, the
paper rose from the ground and began to fly
in the air as it were a bird, at about the
height of a man. Jewād and Iklīl ran after
it, but they had gone scarce forty or fifty
steps when the charm fell to the ground. On
reaching it, they found it burned and reduced
to ashes, whereat Iklīl marvelled. Jewād,
who had brought with him the paper, reed,
and ink, again handed them to Iklīl, and
made him draw from left to right a figure of
steps, then three ovals, then four upright
staves, then four horizontal staves, then one
Solomon's seal. When it was finished, they
placed this paper upon the former burnt
charm, and returned to the tent. Then
Jewād made Iklīl trace the same figures on
another paper and present it all round the
tent and call upon the Spiritual Minister's

name. The moment the number of repetitions was completed, a dreadful crash, like the firing of a mine, was heard, and the ground where lay the charm was blown up, and the earth opened sheer like a cliff. They both went forward and saw an open door through which they entered into an immense cavern filled with silver and gold and jewels and precious things. After carefully examining it all round, they went back to the tent, where Iklīl was made to trace the same figures again, but from right to left ; and they sat down. He was told to recommence the repetition of the Name, and when the number was complete there was a terrific roar like the first, and the place where lay the buried treasure became smooth as before, so that it was irrecognisable ; and Iklīl marvelled exceedingly at these events. A little later the pages and the animals came back ; and they mounted and returned to the imperial palace.

When it was evening and they were left alone, Jewād earnestly addressed Iklīl, saying, 'My Prince, you have this day seen and ascertained that *if it please God (exalted be He!)* it is possible to become through science initiated into the unseen mysteries of Providence ; and that while there are in certain secret places buried treasures whereof none knoweth save the Eternal, it is still conceivable that a knowledge of them may pass to human wisdom through the medium of the Divine Science. Now you will not doubt that it is possible also to discover through this science whether there exist a maiden, chaste, refined, and constant, such as we desire. And he produced the paper, the reed, and the ink-horn, and handed them to Iklīl and said, ' My lord, say in all sincerity of heart, " Doth there exist a lady, modest, honourable, such as is desired ? and, if so, where ? " and then repeat the Noble Verse,

' And with Him are the keys of the unseen,' *

and then breathe upon the reed and draw

* Qur'ān, vi., 59.

four sets of points.'*   After he had made the
points, according to the instructions of Jewād,
he was shown the way of arranging them ;
and, when they were arranged, they saw that
the first figure gave Acquisitio ; the second,
Letitia ; the third, Cauda ; and the fourth,
Populus.   On seeing this, Jewād said, 'My
Prince, good tidings to thee; Acquisitio being
in the first house signifies that the desired
exists.'   When he had made him produce
the other houses according to the rule, he
said, ' Join the second house with the tenth,
and the third with the fourteenth, and then
join the two figures resulting therefrom, and
so produce yet another.'   He did so, and the
figure Puella appeared.   Seeing that Puella
was located in the fifth house, Jewād judged
thus: 'The First Clime is Africa; the Second,
America ; the Third, Europe ; the Fourth,
Persia and Tartary ; the Fifth, Cathay and
China ; this indicates that the desired is in
China ; but in which city ? '   He made Iklīl

* The following ceremony is geomantic.

work the rule for the bearings, and discovered
that the city was Pekin, the capital of the
Empire. He then began to work by another
science, and showed Iklīl the system of the
Circular Table of the Universe, and thus explained it to him : ' My master, Iklīl, the
best branch of the Science of Onomancy is
the beautiful Science of the Circular Table ;
this again consists of two kinds, one of which
is called 'determinative,' and the other 'false-
positive ;' the latter is the simpler, and you
will easily grasp it. First, write down in any
language you please, as if you were asking me,
in what ward is the damsel we seek (we know
her to be in Pekin), and what relation is she
to whom, and what is her name.' Iklīl
wrote down these questions, and Jewād said,
' Separate the letters of the sentence you
have written, and strike out these which
occur more than once, and take those remain-
ing, beginning at the end.' When this was
done eighteen letters remained. ' My lord,'
resumed Jewād, ' in the technical language
of the cabalists are employed phrases figura-

tive in the mysteries of onomancy, such as this,'—and he repeated an incomprehensible Arabic distich, and resumed,—'the sixteenth letter of this distich is the letter of the answer; collect the others in like fashion.' When they had collected them, there resulted the following sentence: *She is the daughter of Lārī, Emperor of China; and they call her name Ferah-Nāz.* And Iklīl perceived the extent of the science and talent of Jewād, and how great a philosopher he was; and he rose and kissed his hand and begged his sublime assistance.

The Real Effectuator planted firmly in a mysterious manner the love of Ferah-Nāz in the heart of Iklīl; and as he yearned and longed for her excessively, imaging her and picturing union with her, the traces of love-longing clouded his perfect beauty, and the sadness of melancholy began to be apparent in the manner of his speech and in the tint of his rosy cheek. One day his father, the King, having perceived the dejection of his son, said to Jewād, 'My life, Jewād Baba,

I like not the appearance of your adopted
brother Iklīl; what has happened to the
Prince, you must surely know?' 'My lord,'
replied Jewād, 'can it be that you have forgotten your imperial command to me to render the Prince desirous of marriage? Com-
plying with your order, I have not only
rendered him desirous of marriage, but have
made him enamoured of an unseen maiden.
What you see is the stress of love.' Then
the King rejoiced as though he had become
lord of all the world, and said, 'My master,
Jewād Baba, may God be pleased with thee;
but would it were not a matter connected
with another clime, whereof the accomplishment is well-nigh impossible.' When the
other replied, 'My lord, it is the daughter of
Lārī Khan, Emperor of the realms of Cathay,'
the King said, 'Alas! we have fallen upon a
great difficulty, our rank will not permit of
our gaining her.' 'My master,' answered
Jewād, 'be calm of heart, your slave is
pledged to unite them; but he begs of you
not to disclose this until the love of the

N

Prince grows ardent, for the ardour of love causeth the endurance of affection and attachment so long as God doth will.' After this conversation with the King, he repaired to the room of Iklīl, whom he thus addressed, ' If you grant permission I shall inform your father of what has passed, and beg him to use his royal endeavour to procure at all hazards Ferah-Nāz.' Iklīl smiled and said, ' My master, Jewād Baba, be kind, there is no use in speaking to my father ; our condition is that of the meanest of the servants of the Emperor ; it were very far from our sphere to endeavour to gain his daughter ; we should only vex and grieve my father to no end.' 'Ah ! my lord,' Jewād answered, ' there is not in this world any affair to which no way exists, nor any business to which no path can be found. Come, then, I will talk for once on the subject with your father.'

So, having forced the Prince's consent, he again entered the presence of the King, and detailed to him the conversation he had held

with Iklīl, and then said, 'My lord, now call
Iklīl and ask him gaily concerning his plight;
and I will show my lord somewhat.' They
sent a man to summon the Prince, whom, on
his entrance, the King motioned to sit respectfully beside Jewād Baba. Then smiling,
according to the injunction, the King thus addressed Iklīl, 'My son, thy adopted brother
has at last turned thee from thy foolish
notions ; although the object of thy desire is
apparently difficult of accomplishment, still
nothing can overcome manly endeavour. *If
it please God (exalted be He!)* we shall ere
long gratify thy wishes.' Iklīl bashful and
confused, was looking straight in front of
him, when Jewād said to the King, 'My lord,
there is indeed no doubt that everything
can ere long be accomplished by your lofty
endeavour ; still it is strange that the Prince
should so fall in love with a being whom he
knows not, and that for one or two tales
and meaningless jests of mine his moon-
bright beauty should be thus dimmed
through longing for her. This morning

I scarce recognised him at first. Dost
thou know what thou art like, my Prince?
Rise and look at thyself for a moment
in that mirror.' And he motioned him
to look in a mirror that was opposite
the King. The King too, following Jewād's
instructions, ordered him to do so, and Iklīl
rose and looked in the mirror, and the moment he did so his appearance and the colour
of his face were altered, and he stood cata-
leptic like a Sa'dī dervish.* When the King
saw this plight of his darling, he said in the
greatest consternation, 'What has befallen
thee?' 'O my lord,' replied the Prince,
'I saw in the mirror that very damsel whom
I beheld in my vision long ago.' And the
King and the Prince were bewildered and
looked in the face of Jewād. And Jewād
thus addressed Iklīl, 'My Prince, that maiden
whom thou sawest is the daughter of the
Emperor; *if it please God (exalted be He!)*,

* A dervish of the order founded by Sa'du-'d-Dīn el-
Jebāvī.

I shall ere long gratify thy wishes ; but till
I come beware that thou do nothing in this
matter, and vex not thy heart, be assured
that the maiden shall be thine.' So saying,
Jewād vanished from before the King and
Prince, leaving them both plunged in amazement.

When Jewād disappeared from before the
King and Prince he went to the city of
Pekin, where he changed his appearance and
assumed that of a heathen priest. Now, they
had in that city a false god called the Great
Kisa, a mighty idol, a monster about the size
of Leander's Tower,* some two hundred
cubits high. At each corner of his temple
was a column, and between each of the four
columns was hung a curtain of Cathayan
gold-brocade ; round the curtains was a space
ten cubits wide, which, instead of being paved
with marble, was covered with fire, and all
round the fire there was a moat of water,
thirty cubits wide. This water was always

* At Constantinople.

boiling, but its heat was not as that of ordinary warm water, for if a piece of wood or a
stone were thrown therein, it at once melted
it and caused it to disappear, as nitric
acid corrodes, but more quickly. All round
about this lake were erected strange and
wonderful buildings; those were numerous
temples where thousands of priests were engaged in worshipping from a distance the idol
which was behind the curtain. They called
the chief priest the Per-No-Per, and he was
more revered by them than the Emperor
himself.

Jewād, having discovered this by his
science, went straight to the temple of the
Chief Priest and entered the room where he
was; and, enquiring for his health and circumstances, after the fashion of an equal,
passed up and seated himself. The Priest,
seeing the youth of Jewād and his unmannerly conduct, waxed exceeding wroth and
said, 'Who art thou, and what art thou, and
whence art thou?' 'I am of China,' replied Jewād, 'and am come at the summons

of the Great Kisa ; last night while I was worshipping alone, the Great Kisa appeared to me and said, " I have chosen thee to be my guardian, do thou come into my presence; and tell the man who is now the Per-No-Per that by reason of his great age he must yield to thee his office and retire into the corner of seclusion. If he obey not this order he shall become the object of my wrath and fury. Should he ask of thee, he has committed such and such a sin at such and such a time in such and such a place, and to gain pardon for that crime he held up his left hand for twelve years, and was forgiven ; no person knows these things, only I and he. This is proof enough ; let him credit thee." ' The poor old man, quaking and trembling, rose and swept the dust at Jewād's feet with his white beard and said, ' My master, what is your command ? I shall this moment arise and go whithersoever you order me.' ' No,' answered Jewād, ' thou art an acceptable servant of the Great Idol, having been so many years in his service, we shall remain

together ; but now go thou to the Emperor
and the other great men and tell them all to
assemble here on the morrow; for the Great
Kisa has ordered that they all be here when
I go into his presence.' 'Most willingly,'
said the old man, and having laid his face in
the dust, he went to summon them.

This wonderful event was noised through
the city ; and in the morning all assembled,
and the Emperor and the army stood respectfully, observing the beauty of Jewād. Taking
the old Per-No-Per to his side, Jewād said,
'Let us pray to the Great Kisa ;' and while
he was passing through the throng of people
to the water's edge, he saw that Ferah-Nāz
was standing by her father's side looking on.
When he reached the water Jewād raised his
hands as if he were praying, while in reality
he was invoking many a curse on the vile
soul of the infamous sorcerer who had made
the Kisa. They saw a part of the curtain
drawn aside and a terrible dragon, such as
may not be pictured or imagined, emerged.
It came straight up to Jewād and said, 'My

master, if your leave be granted, I shall
devour the daughter of the Emperor.'
'Nay,' was the reply, 'until I have gone
into the presence of the Image and learned
her crime thou shalt do her no hurt; return
to thy place ;' and he sent it back.   Thereupon there came from the place of the Kisa
a richly-caparisoned horse ; when it stood by
Jewād's side he gracefully mounted it, and
while he was riding on he said to the old
priest, 'Go, tell the Emperor to take that
vain girl hence and let her not stand there in
front of the Kisa.'   Having thus warned him,
Jewād rose into the air, and when he came
near to the curtain it opened of its own accord and he entered and it closed again.
And the folk stared with wonder at these
strange events.

In the meantime the old priest went to the
Emperor and said, 'For Heaven's sake, stay
not here, take away that vain creature, thy
daughter, and begone.   Didst not thou see
the dragon and hear the reason of its coming ? '   When he had related the whole

incident, the unhappy Emperor returned to his palace with fear and trembling. These events well nigh turned the people of the city from their old faith and made them invest Jewād with divinity ; and the cries of 'ezin-ku-per,' which in the language of Cathay means *extolled be the perfection of God*, and the peals of the bells which were tolled in the temples ascended to the star Capella. When two hours had elapsed, Jewād returned as before and descended with dignity from the horse which went back again. And Jewād came and sat in his place, and the folk advanced in companies and rubbed their faces in the dust at his feet, and gave him joy of his return, and showered upon him sequins and jewels innumerable.

That night passed, and when it was morning a servant of the Emperor came and said, 'If the permission of the Per-No-Per be granted, the Emperor seeks leave to come and kiss the dust at his feet.' As he granted permission, though assuming indifference, the Emperor came with great humility and rubbed his face in the dust at Jewād's feet, and humbly begged forgiveness for his past sins. Comforting the Emperor and treating him with kindness, Jewād said, 'The god is well pleased with thee because thou art a wise and merciful Emperor, and has forgiven all of thy faults; but thy daughter is living in mighty sin, and I much entreated the Great Kisa and have saved her from his fury.' Then the Emperor wept much and bitterly and said, 'My master, whatsoever her sin be, she shall turn from it and repent ; or, if it be possible to expiate it by lavishing treasure, I shall thus seek its pardon ;' and he clasped the feet of Jewād. 'Send word to Ferah-Nāz that she come, and we shall see ; if she repent, her pardon is probable,' was the reply. So Ferah-Nāz was summoned into the presence of Jewād. When she came she made to fall at the feet of the Per-No-Per, but he cried harshly and sternly, 'Hold! approach me not, it is grievous sin even to look on the face of a sinner like to thee.' When he said this, the peerless frame of

Ferah-Nāz, formed of the young rose-leaf, trembled as though seized with fever, and she fell to weeping. Jewād had become acquainted through spiritual means with all that had occurred during the conversations between the Princess and Libāba, so he addressed the Emperor thus : 'Though few have been created like this thy daughter, a possessor of honour and a lady of refinement, yet by reason of a certain evil notion she has become more guilty in the eyes of the Great Kisa than all the other women in the world. Her sin is this : having seen a vision, she refuses to have any intercourse with men ; and howsoever much her nurse has counselled her she still remains obstinate and positive. If this obstinacy should spread to other women and they acquire the custom of not marrying, it will be the cause of the extinction of the worshippers of the Great Kisa ; that is her sin.' Then turning to Ferah-Nāz, he said, 'Dost not thou know that the interpretation of a vision is the opposite of what is seen, not the very thing itself ? Why

didst not thou make the male deer the
female, and the female the male ? There is
no constancy in those ; what madman ever
believed that it existed in scheming women ?
That fair youth whom thou sawest in the
vision is Iklīlu-'l-Mulk, son of the King of
Cashmere ; the Great Kisa has given thee to
him, and if thou accept him not from heart
and soul, thou shalt repent it.' The poor
Emperor, who, imagining his daughter's sin
to be something reflecting on her honour,
had been ashamed, was overcome with joy
and delight on hearing those words, and
kissed the feet of Jewād. His daughter too
repented of her sin from the depths of her
heart ; and, having beheld the beauty of the
Prince in her vision, she declared that she
accepted him from heart and soul, and said
that if it were ordered her she should walk
forthwith all the way to Cashmere and kiss
the dust at his feet. Jewād, altering his
manner, said, ' Well done, my daughter, see,
how this will please the Great Kisa ! But
departure is dependant on his will ; let them

provide thee with a private room, and there
for a few days occupy thyself with worship
along with thy nurse Libāba, all of whose
sins are pardoned for her having exhorted
thee, and who is a most acceptable servant of
the Kisa. After that we shall see what the
god will ordain.' Then Ferah-Nāz kissed
the ground before Jewād and returned joyous
to her private room ; and the Emperor also
went to his palace with a happy heart.

When Jewād had thus gained his object
and secured his treasure, he thought in himself, 'Although her conversion is of those
things possible at any time, yet it were not
well to bring her in this heathenism ; it were
better to convert her here.' Having thus
decided, two days afterwards he called Ferah-
Nāz before him and received her with much
kindness and rejoiced her by telling her that
all her sins were pardoned, and said, ' Thou
canst not conceive how I am pleased at thy
thus repenting and loving Iklīl in sincerity ;
above all, the Great Kisa, besides forgiving
all thy faults, has deemed thee worthy an

honour never till this moment granted any
person: he has commanded thee to be brought
into his presence ; come, let us go.' And he
took her hand, and when they came to the
edge of that dread and terrible water, he said,
' My daughter, Ferah-Nāz, let not my robe
slip from thy hand, and fear nothing and
follow me ;' and he began to walk upon the
water. Ferah-Nāz, too, gathering courage,
stepped upon the water, and when she per=-
ceived that it was as if she trod upon a lawn,
without fear and without dismay she passed
to the fire ; and not only had the fire no
effect upon her, but she felt not even the
slightest heat therefrom. They came to the
curtain and Jewād raised it, and they passed
within. Ferah-Nāz looked and saw that
there was behind the curtain nought save an
empty space, and she asked, 'Where is the
Great Kisa?' 'Sit down and I shall tell
thee,' said Jewād, and he seated her and sat
down beside her, and thus spoke : ' My
daughter, for many thousand years has thy
nation been deceived by this strange sorcery,

blindly believing in a false god behind this
curtain.   The Absolute Deity who hath
created this earth and these heavens and thee
and me and all men and all worlds is unfet-
tered by the conditions of place and space.
Just as the soul is surely existent in
the human body and yet can have no
special place assigned to it, so is the True
Deity, who is the Creator of all beings, ex-
empt from any definite locality.   And like
as the soul is unable to be seen, so, too, is the
True Deity invisible.   But as speech and the
motions of the body are signs and proofs
that the soul is present in the body, so do
the revolutions and motions of the planets
and the spheres, and the rotation of the four
seasons, and the growth and decay of all
creatures, show that this world has a Creator
and a Lord.   And many other signs there
are ; yea, every atom is a witness, if thou but
consider it.   And the universe is not merely
this world which thou dost see ; as while
asleep we wander in the world of dreams, so
when we die must we pass to another world,

which they call the World of the Hereafter.
Then shall all those who have believed in
that Deity be blessed in bowers and gardens
amid joys and pleasures innumerable, such
as eyes have not seen or ears heard, and
which fade not away or vanish, but are eternal. But those who trust in lies and sorceries
like this Kisa must enter then a fire, not like
the false fire of this Kisa, but such that if a
single spark therefrom were to fall upon the
earth, it would reduce the whole world to
ashes. That fire they call Hell. But we
have not found this sure and certain knowledge through our own learning ; a beloved
one, faithful and upright, called Muhammed,
came from that True Deity and taught us ;
and we know and believe him to be true. It
is by reason of my greatly loving thee that I
have brought thee here, that thou might
know this place to be void and turn from
this idolatry. My suffering no hurt from the
sorceries of this Kisa, and my knowing what
thou sawest in that vision, and my compre-
hending many thousand things unseen, and

my being able to nullify and set aside these
falsities, are through my believing in that
True Deity, whose glorious name is God, and
through my acknowledging and confessing
Muhammed, His Beloved. Thou too, if thou
believe that there is in the heavens and the
earth no other god than that God, and that
whatsoever Muhammed, His Beloved, hath
said is right and true, shalt attain to those
eternal joys and shalt be, like me, able to
annul such sorceries and to know things unseen.   But, if thou believe not my words,
thou must without doubt remain for ever in
the fire.'

When Ferah-Nāz, whose wisdom and up-
rightness have been mentioned in her conversation with her nurse, heard from Jewād
these words of guidance, she fell at his feet
and thus made confession, ' It is not unknown to the God of whom you speak that
from the time when I attained to discretion,
I have known the rites of the idolators to be
vain through this reasoning, that although
this perilous sea is wondrous when beheld,

there is many and many a realm far from
here, the people of which know not even the
name thereof; yet bread is provided to those
people from the unseen world. Thus considered, it is clear that the truth concerning
this Kisa is that it is vanity and enchantment. Thus have I ever thought: praise be
to God that by your aid I have solved the
problem.' When she had become a Muslim
by repeating the Two Words of the Profession, she said, 'Things are so; but you, my
master, who are you?' So he told her that
his name was Jewād, and all about how he
had come on purpose to take her to Iklīl.
She asked, 'O my master, how shall we go?'
And Jewād answered her, 'Do thou go out
from here and fear not the fire and the water,
henceforward such enchantments can have
no effect on thee. Go straight to thy father
and tell him that I brought thee hither, and
that after my entrance here the Great Kisa
will never give me leave to come forth, and
that the Image has ordered him to send thee
this day to Cashmere. I now go thither,

and, *if it please God*, I will come forth to
meet thee with the troops when thou arrivest.
But should they ask thee what the image is
like, answer that it is unlawful to describe it,
and let not anyone discover the secret.'

So saying he sent Ferah-Nāz to her father,
and transported himself to the door of the
King's room in Cashmere. By happy chance
Iklīl was in the presence of the King, and
they were talking about Jewād when he
entered. 'Thank God!' he cried, and he
paid the respects due to royalty, and the King
and Iklīl both rose to welcome him, manifest-
ing great delight. But Iklīl trembled, for it
was only five days since he had started, and
he feared some obstacle had arisen which
had occasioned his return. Jewād comprehended his thoughts and said, 'O my Prince,
be happy. I have constrained Ferah-Nāz to
love thee, and she is coming here desiring
union with thee;' and he related everything
as it had happened. And they both of them
wondered and marvelled, and they perceived
what manner of man was Jewād, though in

appearance but a dervish. Although the King was pleased at the joy of his son, he dreaded the power and might of Jewād, and a fear such as this took possession of his heart: 'should he be in any way offended with us, it is certain that in a single moment he could give our kingdom and our life to the winds.' So assuming great politeness, he said, as if ashamed of his past conduct, 'Pray come up here, my master,' and motioned to a place at his side. Jewād, by his divine insight, perceived what was passing in the mind of the King, and, smiling, answered, ·' No, my lord, this sort of conduct is a scolding of your servant. I am your slave. It is not right that my master's royal heart should be changed towards me because of my displaying a few Bektāshī tricks. I beg that you doubt not that Providence in appointing me for your glorious service means to bless your royal heart, and that you believe me to be among the meanest of your slaves, howsoever much I may be unworthy of that honour. But if you are going to consider me a magic-

working scoundrel, who, if he be not honoured
and flattered, will play you some trick, tell
me so at once, there is no need of ceremony,
and I shall be off and away to some other
land.' The King was amazed at this knowledge and penetration of Jewād, and he
strained him to his bosom and received him
as a son in no wise differing from Iklīl, and
swore by God the Most High Ruler never
again to cease from trusting him. And
Jewād likewise promised henceforward to
accept Hurmuz Shah in all respects as his
true father and Iklīl as his dear brother; and
they grasped one another's hands and spliced
the bond of paternity and fraternity ; and
their hearts were filled with joy.

Two or three days afterwards when Iklīl
was with Jewād he began to recite the chorus:

'Alas ! alas ! my love, my life, when is it thou wilt
    come ? '

to which Jewād, to console him, answered
with the song :

'Be patient, heart, one day shalt thou to thy desire
    attain.'

Another day when Jewād and Iklīl were
seated in the presence of the King, engaged
in mystic.converse and spiritual diversion,
one of the ministers entered bearing a document. When the King had made himself
aware of its contents the colour of his face
changed, and he handed it to Jewād, who
looked at it and saw that they had written
thereon that Qara Khan the King of the
Moguls, an ancient enemy, had now crossed
the frontier with an army greater than the
land could hold and, by hurrying as if on a
foray, had approached to within three days'
journey of the capital. Jewād gave back the
document to the King and smiled, whereupon the latter said, ' My dear, this is no
affair of mirth, the foe is mighty ; what is
your advice in this matter ? ' On help and
aid being thus sought from him, Jewād replied, ' My King, my lord, seeing that God
who maketh hard things easy hath given thee
a son like Jewād, it is not right that thou be
anxious over an evident plaything such as
this. To-morrow, *if it please God (exalted be*

He!), order thou a levée to be held in such and such a pavilion by the city gate; an opportunity for a fine spectacle has arisen. But, my lord, my brother's patience and repose have departed—he will not accept comfort; it cannot be helped though, the cause being a maid, my King.' When he had thus jestingly changed the subject, the King was assured of his might and power and was comforted. But still the human nature is wonderful, he could not dismiss the idea of external means and outward causes, so he again betrayed his anxiety by saying, 'Is no preparation of the appliances of defence necessary? Let us at least order the generals and officers to get ready the troops they have at hand.' 'No, my Sovereign,' answered Jewād, 'summon now your minister and instruct him how that the people are to put on their best clothes and adorn themselves as they do at the Festival and the New Year, how that nothing of the nature of a weapon of war is to be worn by any person, and how that they are to range themselves.

outside the city gate. Though the minister should appear dismayed, pay thou no attention to his promptings and suggestions.' Having thus instructed the King, he went with Iklīl to his own room, where they gave themselves up to mirth.

So the minister was summoned, and when he heard from the King these orders like a hashish-eater's dream, he was confounded, and returned and sat down in his place and thus thought, ' There must be some vision which the eyes of that man can see, otherwise there were no use of such instructions : *I extol the perfection of God: There is no strength nor any power saving in God.'* So he assembled all the officers and grandees of the State, and began his address with the noble verse, ' *Verily we belong unto God,'** and when he had explained what were the orders of the King, surprise fell upon every one and they despaired of their lives, and each retired and wept.

* Qur'ān, ii., 151.

Two days afterwards the levée was held
according to the instructions of Jewād, and
while the grandees and the vezirs and the
officers and the ministers and all were eagerly
watching the road, they saw an ass upon
which was a man whose two hands were
firmly tied to the pommel of the saddle, and
a lad twelve years old led the animal by the
headstall. Behind the ass came four men
bound with chains, their hands manacled behind their backs; after these came other four
bound men, with chains round their necks
joining them with the first four; behind those
came others, and so on till twelve thousand
men all bound with chains passed like a file
of cranes. Great terror fell upon the people,
and while they were gazing, wondering what
it could be, Jewād whispered in the ear of
the King, 'Lo, the man on the ass is Qara
Khan; send your minister to welcome him
and bring him before you; lodge the rest,
fettered, in prison.' 'Who is the lad who
leads the ass?' asked the King. 'My lord,'
answered Jewād, 'he is one of the slaves in

the service of your slave ; I sent that child
out last night and he has bound all that
army.' Then said the King addressing the
minister, 'Dost thou see the mercy of God?
Thanks be to Him ; he who is on the ass is
our enemy Qara Khan ; go, bring him before
us.'

So the Vezir went and met Qara Khan
and loosed his bonds and brought him to the
King. He omitted nought of the honours
due to kings ; and Hurmuz Shah said to
him with dignity, 'What is this?' 'Last
night,' replied Qara Khan, 'great fatigue fell
upon myself and my army, and we slept
heavily ; when it was morning we found ourselves upon the road fettered in this fashion.
I know not what is the cause thereof ; but it
would seem to be a punishment for my
having meditated evil against thee without
provocation, a sign of the might of the
Merciful Ruler.' Hurmuz Shah replied to
comfort him, 'Very good, your confession
of your sin is an indication that henceforward
you will live peaceably.' And they each

mounted a royal steed and rode side by
side to the palace. That night there was a
regal banquet; and on the morrow, according to Jewād's instructions, a high divan was
held. Two thrones were erected in the place
of honour, and the Kings sat side by side.
Hurmuz Shah then called to him the Chief
Preceptor and said, 'Interrogate my brother,
Qara Khan, concerning the peace and alliance
that is between us; and write down what he
says.' When Qara Khan was asked, that
poor man, knowing not what he ought to
say, rose and held up his hands before
the divan and made answer, ' People of
Muhammed, bear witness that henceforward
I and my children's children gird the loins
of obedience to the commands of Hurmuz
Shah and his children's children. If I depart
from this pledge, or if any of my children
rebel against this house, may we be the
objects of the wrath of God, and disgraced
in this world and in that to come.' When
he had uttered these words in a loud voice,
they were written in gold upon a paper,

which was handed to Hurmuz Shah, who
said, 'O my King, I beg that you will rest
at ease for a few days our guest ; but order
your troops to take their tents and baggage
back from the place where they now are to
your capital ; and retain here only your
private attendants.' So all Qara Khan's
soldiers and servants were liberated ; and
after they had been treated with feasts for
a day or two, Hurmuz Shah instructed his
minister to see about their departure ; thus,
having got rid of the presence of the troops,
they passed each day with joy and pleasure
in some charming spot or promenade.

Let us go to Ferah-Nāz : she went forth
from the Kisa, and, having without fear
passed over the fire and the water, came to
her father's palace and met with her parents.
When she had told the Emperor that the
Per-No-Per was going to remain in the presence of the image, and that he had ordered
the old Per-No-Per to be reinstated, and
herself to set out in three days' time for
Cashmere, and had given him some other

messages, he wondered and marvelled at
the case of the priest. And straightway he
made preparations for the road, and gave
her, by way of dower, countless rarities and
curiosities worth the world, which for these
many thousand years had been being collected in the treasuries of Cathay, and appointed some thousands of horsemen and
footmen as guards, and sent her to the bridal
bower, the city of Cashmere. When she was
come near that city, private emissaries informed Jewād, who with a grand array went
forth to meet the bride. Jewād was para-
nymph; and for forty days they feasted and
made merry, and they married Iklīl and
Ferah-Nāz, and grafted those two fair trees
of the garden of the earth.

One day, while the mirth and merriment
were yet going on, the guest Qara Khan,
observing the regal attention shown to Jewād
in the presence of the King, and imagining
that Hurmuz Shah was fond of dervishes,
and that that person was his sheykh, but
thinking that even were such the case, it

was unbecoming that one so young should
be the guide and director of an old man,
said to the King, 'My lord, surely yonder
dervish is of your kindred.' The King
replied, 'My lord, he is my son, who prayeth
for you; but judge not of him by the fewness
of his years: he studies spiritual sciences and
chooses to wear that form.' 'Very good,
my lord,' answered he ; and then addressing
Jewād with much affection, said, 'Son, I
much love dervishes ; indeed my Kingship—
which now I owe to the pardon and kindness
of this monarch of lofty rank—is the blessing
arising from the noble words of an honoured
saint ; if the King grant permission, I shall
relate the story.' Leave having been given,
he thus began the tale of his adventures :—

THE STORY OF QARA KHAN.

" I am a native of Basra. Being a poor
man, I became, through reason of my
poverty, a sailor in one of the ocean ships,
and in that manner I gained my livelihood.

After many other voyages, we went to New
Holland, and on our return, when we were
over against the island of Ceylon, we encountered a great storm, so that we ran on
for five days and nights, it being impossible
to look at the chart or compass. On the
sixth day the hurricane abated, and we had
not gone far ere the wind fell altogether, and
the calm was such that even a twig would
have lain motionless upon the sea. The
master took the astrolabe in his hand, and
looked at the sun ; he found that we had
deviated twenty-one degrees from our course,
so, according to the reckoning that every
degree is sixty-six and two-thirds miles, we
were 1350 miles astray ; but as we had no
register we were ignorant as to what longi-
tude we were in. While we were thinking of
these things the ship began to move although
there was no wind, and her speed gradually
increased to such a rate that favouring
breezes could not have borne her along so
quickly ; and we all marvelled at this. In
the course of two hours we could discern a

shore, and a little afterwards we reached it. The vessel came upon the shore broadside on, and we saw her cleave thereto as though she had been fastened to it by a thousand nails. Crying ' *We extol the perfection of God!*' we all streamed out ; but what did we see ? —the shore was composed of mountains of loadstone ; and then we knew that to be the reason of the vessel's advancing with so great rapidity. But there was no help for it. We all assembled together and consulted, and we came to the conclusion that there was no resource but that each should go in a different direction and see if he could find any village or road, and should return in the evening and inform his comrades.

" So we each set out, with this purpose, in a different direction to seek and search. In that which I went was a high hill. Thinking to myself that it were better to climb to the top of this mountain and look around than wander vacantly in the plain, I ascended to the summit, heeding not the fatigue. I saw there a temple ; I gave God thanks thinking

P

it an omen of good; but looking round I
could see no signs of habitation. I entered
the temple, it was empty, but a drum and a
stick were hanging on one wall and opposite
them was a tablet. I approached and saw '
inscribed thereon in a beautiful hand in the
Persian language: 'O ye shipmen who hap-
pen here! be it known unto you that hence
is no escape. I, who am Zābir of the children of Jupiter, versed in magic and enchantments: an adverse wind having cast me
here, I have raised this building as my monu-
ment and have placed herein this talisman,
by means of which, if any man of a ship's
company that falleth into this woe consent
through zeal and love of God to sacrifice
himself that he may save the rest, he may
avail thereto. Let all the travellers enter the
ship, and when all is ready let that self-sacrificer come here and strike this drum with
the stick three times: at the first stroke the
ship shall be removed from this place as far
as the sight can reach, at the second stroke
to a distance of five hundred miles, at the

third stroke they shall gain a place of safety.'
When I had read this and understood it, I
sped back with haste to the vessel's side, and,
having discovered that none of the others
had any information, I mentioned the drum
and the stick and the writing on the tablet.
We all sat down together and deliberated.
Each said, 'After I am dead what matter is
the safety of the rest to me ? If we must die,
let us die together.' I saw that none of them
had zeal enough for this deed, so I thus addressed them, 'Brothers, since we have made
sure of death in this place, now is the Hereafter at hand for us and the world afar ; is
not it needful at last to prepare for the Hereafter?   I will sacrifice myself for the love of
God ; do ye rise and enter the ship.'

"Taking some bread and a skin full of
water, I went to the place of the drum, and,
heeding not the suggestions of Satan, struck
it with the stick as soon as I entered.   I went
forth and saw that the ship was no longer in
her place, but far out at sea.   I entered again
and twice struck the drum with the stick ;

and went out and saw that the ship was wholly lost to view, and I knew that they were in safety. Swinging the skin on to my back, I went down the other side of the hill, and after I had wandered on for ten days the sea again appeared before my eyes, and I knew that the place was an island. When I reached the shore I sat down, and as the bread and water were finished I awaited the coming of death. While lying on the margin of the ocean, it came into my mind how it was better to die in the sea than on the land; and, having a little strength left, and knowing that an effort to save one's self in the deep is the cause of a reward in the other world,* I blew out the empty skin and firmly tied its mouth. Mounting upon it as on a horse, I launched myself out into the sea and began to move my legs like oars. Now, just as the property of the one side of the loadstone was attraction, that of the other was repulsion; I had

* A person who has been drowned is considered a martyr.

a key with me, and I saw that the speed of
the skin was quicker than that of a six-oared
boat. Its speed gradually increased, and at
the end of two hours I perceived a shore.
When I had arrived thereat, I landed and I
saw that it was a place like a false Paradise,
adorned with various sorts of trees and
numerous streams and all kinds of fruits. I
bowed my face to the ground, and ate of the
fruits and satisfied my hunger, and drank of
the sweet water of the streams and gave
thanks and praise to God.

"As night came on, I laid myself in a corner and went to sleep. When it was morning, I rose again and ate some fruits, and
went along, following the course of a stream,
and I found every spot to be beautiful and
charming. Having ascended a hill, I saw
before me in the distance in the middle of a
plain a vast dome covered with gold. 'Praise
be to God!' I cried, 'I doubt not but that is
the sign of deliverance ; but the presence of
a golden dome in the midst of an empty
plain like yon is remote from reason ; is it a

magic phantom, or what is it? But whatever
it be it would not do but to go to it.' So I
went to the dome and found it to be a building such that if all the kings of the earth
were to assemble together for the purpose,
they could not produce one stone like those
of which it was constructed : that description
is sufficient.   I went three times round its
four sides, but could discover no trace of
door or window, and while I was looking
at it in bewilderment, I saw a man
in the distance beckoning me with his
hand to come to him.   I at once went to
him ; he was a grey-bearded qalender, and
he said, 'Come, brother, you are welcome.'
We sat down in the shade of a tree, and he
drove away my fears by his great kindness.
He then took from his wallet a warm nicely
cooked fowl, and a loaf of fine bread ; these
he placed before me telling me to eat them.
I ate the whole of the fowl and the bread,
and satisfied myself and praised God, and I
asked out of gratitude, 'My saint, who are
you and what manner of place is that?'

'Son,' answered he, 'that place is the holy
tomb of Our Lord Imām Muhammed Bāqir,*
the descendant of the pure Prophet ; and I
am of its guardians and attendants. God's
bringing thee hither is because of His satisfaction with thee for thy sacrificing of thyself.'
When the dervish said this I was amazed at
his penetration. About an hour afterwards
he asked me, saying, 'O brother, dost thou
now desire to go?' 'Where should I go?'
I asked. 'To thine own country,' he replied.
'Thou shalt pass beyond that hill and go on,'
said he ; and he gave me a tablet of Chinese
jade, about the size of the palm of the hand,
engraven with strange characters. Then he
continued, 'Wear it upon thy head, and by
the virtue of this tablet thou shalt wear a
kingly crown ; the tablet itself shall surely
reach him whom I intend.'

"I placed the tablet upon my head, and
thereupon a giddiness came over me, and I
shut my eyes ; I wished myself in Basra, and

* The Fifth Imām.

I found myself sitting in my mother's house. Ere long the ship with my companions returned ; and they were astonished at finding me in Basra, and asked concerning my adventures. I told them that there was a harbour on the other side of the island, and that I had got on board a ship and come. From that time the Lord Most High has given me ease of circumstances and abundance of wealth ; day by day these increased till the extent of my riches reached such a degree that it was the cause of a dispute with the King of Basra. I fled with many men to the country of the Moguls, and stretched forth my hand on every side ; and at last, behold, I am, thank God, King of the Moguls. Look you, son, that is how a dervish ought to be."

Jewād said, ' My lord, is it possible to see that tablet ?' ' Surely, surely,' replied Qara Khan, and he unrolled his turban ; upon his cap was a purse firmly sewed up. He ripped open the purse and handed the tablet to

Jewād, who looked at it with attention and saw the following written upon it in the basil hand :* 'O my brother Jewād, the Divine Knowledge is not to be gained by viewing the circumstances of the earth ; the travel of the Mystic Journey is a boundless ocean, the shore of which not even the Prophets have been able to reach, as is attested by the pearl-scattering words, ' *Glory be to Thee !— We have not known Thee according to the due of thine acquaintanceship.*'† After thousands of years of travel through the climes of truths and the plains of the exposition of subtleties' all that thou wouldst see would be thine own art or thine own knowledge. Waste not time ; restrain thyself from looking at thyself, and draw tight the girdle of endurance to reach the realm of dissolution.

> Light thy heart then with that brilliant radiancy :
> How long wilt thou lick the plate of 'Bū-'Alī?‡

---

* *Reyhānī*, a sort of ornamental hand-writing, said to be so named because of the resemblance of the pen with which it is written to the leaf of the sweet basil.

† This is a Hadīs, or traditional saying of the Apostle.

‡ 'Bū-'Alī for Ebū-'Alī, his teacher.

Success in this matter is dependent on seeking inspiration with pure belief. *And peace
is on him who followeth direction.'*

When Jewād understood the meaning of
what was written on the tablet, he uttered a
great cry ; and he restored it to Qara Khan.
Hurmuz Shah and Iklīl asked the reason of
the cry, and he replied :

> ' That same moment when I washed me at the fountain
>   pure of Love,
> Over the Two Worlds and all things I the burial-service
>   read.*

O my master, you ask of its reason and its
cause ; travel is now incumbent on your
slave.' And he embraced the King and
Iklīl and bade them farewell. Then he went
to his room, and with joy performed the
ablution and sat upon the prayer-mat and
repeated this supplication : *'O Helper of
understanding ; and no one attaineth to understanding unless Thou perfect his understanding. And O Viewer of the heart ; and its*

---

* *i.e.,* When I was filled with the Divine Love I gave up
all thought alike for this world and the next.

knowledge sufficeth not unless Thou make sufficient its inspiration. And O Thou Present to every existent thing; and there is no existent thing, unless lost in the necessity of His existence.' And he laid his head on the pillow of seeking inspiration.

Straightway he opened his eyes, and he found himself lying on a shore near a vast city, a mighty capital. He rose, and wondering, said in himself, ' My life, I was in my room in such and such a place, this that is before me resembles not our city. *There is no strength nor any power, saving in God.* Am I in a vision?' In a single moment poor Jewād forgot all that he knew—those spiritual sciences and strange arts that he had learned and practised for so long, all his wisdom and attainments, his manifest gifts, his initiation into the arcana ; nay, even what he had learned and comprehended through his five outer and inner human senses ; and he stood as though new born from his mother, staring all around him in confusion. He saw a person of seemingly

threescore-and-five years, and he said to him,
'My life, my good father, what manner of
city is this, and who are you?' The man
replied, 'They call this city the City of
Belovedness,* and my name is Hāfiz Mustafa; I am of the inhabitants of the city, a
poor man, one who has abandoned the world.
But thou seemest to be a stranger?' Jewād
answered, 'Yes, I am of the city of Athens.'
Then the man said, 'Since thou art a
stranger, come with me to my private
house;' and he took Jewād by the hand,
and they entered the city. It was a
city, the stones and blocks of all the
gates and walls and houses of which were of
red ruby, even the flags wherewith it was
paved were of pomegranate-coloured ruby,
and engraven with beautiful characters; so
that it were impossible for one in a thousand
years to complete the study of the Divine
Mysteries which the art of the Sempiternal
had written upon its every stone, and upon

* Mahbūbiyya.

every leaf of its every tree. But what could
poor Jewād do? That time was not the
time for study, and his skill in deciphering
had passed away. They somehow reached
that person's dwelling ; as he was of those
who had abandoned the world, there were no
ceremonial restraints in his house ; it was a
house so free of ceremony that it were impossible to describe it ; yet the meanest of
its countless servants could have made a
beggar a Korah* and a King of the Kings
of the earth. After resting a little the man
said, ' O son, as you have come to our city,
it is necessary you go before our King.'
And he took Jewād by the hand and led
him to the palace of the King. The appearance of the palace, and the splendour of the
courtiers, and the magnificence of the divan,
may be judged from the circumstances of a
poor man of the city. The hapless Jewād
had left him no eye to see, or understanding

* Korah, like Crœsus, typifies an enormously wealthy
man.

to observe, or comprehension to know, or tongue to speak. When he entered the Royal presence and raised his eyes to look upon the beauty of the King, he saw that he who sat upon the indescribable throne was—HIMSELF.

Temma-'l-Kitāb
Bi-'awni-'llāhi-'l-Wahhāb.